PUNK ROCK DAD

Collins
An Imprint of HarperCollinsPublishers

PUNK ROCK DAD

NO RULES, JUST REAL LIFE

JIM LINDBERG

HarperCollins books may be purchased for educational, business, or sales promotional use. For information, please write: Special Markets Department, HarperCollins Publishers, 10 East 53rd Street, New York, NY 10022.

FIRST EDITION

Designed by Sunil Manchikanti

Library of Congress Cataloging-in-Publication Data
  Jim Lindberg.
        Punk rock dad : no rules, just real life / Jim Lindberg.—1st ed.
          p.   cm.
        Contents: Story of my life—Party at Ground Zero—Hey, ho! Let's go!—Mommy's little monster—Anarchy in the pre-K—We're a happy family—F@#K authority?
      ISBN 978-0-06-114875-0
      ISBN-10: 0-06-114875-X
        1. Linderg, Jim. 2. Pennywise (Musical group) 3. Punk rock musicians—California—Biography. 4. Fathers—California—Biography. I. Title.
  ML420.L7115A3 2007
  782.42166092—dc22
      [B]   2006051732

07 08 09 10 11 ❖/RRD 10 9 8 7 6 5 4 3 2 1

for my girls

CONTENTS

INTRO

PARENTS' NIGHT

We recently had parents' night at our kids' school, which is usually a lot of fun for a punk rock dad. This is when the school has the parents come in so they can prove to you they've actually been teaching your kids something and not just locking them up in a closet somewhere after you've dropped them off. Daughter number two's preschool class had a project for Father's Day where each four-year-old child came to class dressed like their dad at work, in his own actual clothes, to have their picture taken by the teacher. The other dads and I filed in and politely shuffled by the row of our daughters' portraits, which were neatly lined up on a table beneath the chalkboard in the classroom. Most of the little girls in the pictures were wearing a suit and tie like their businessman or lawyer dads, some were in fireman or paramedic uniforms, and a few were in construction worker's or plumber's clothes. Last in line, on the very end, was my daughter, proudly holding my beaten-up electric guitar, which was painted in silver sparkles, emblazoned with various offensive decals, and held together by duct tape. She was wearing my torn up jeans and black hi-tops, her hair was tucked up under the tattered green and white trucker hat I always wear, and draped across her tiny frame was my faded red T-shirt that looked like it had a Nike logo across the front, but instead of the company name, it said "RIOT!"

Needless to say, our picture got the most comments out of the class projects, with the dads chortling and guffawing and pointing it out to other guys in line. At that moment I wasn't sure if I should be proud or if I should punch someone.

This is pretty much the case whenever the parents get together for an official or unofficial school function. At PTA meetings, award ceremonies, T-ball games, and Christmas parties, the first question out of everyone's mouth when you meet someone new in the parenting world is, "So what do you do?" The acceptable and consistently offered responses are usually, "I'm a lawyer," or "stockbroker," or "account executive." It's usually some very official, very important-sounding position at a major law firm or huge corporation involved in world domination. When I have to respond with what I do for a living, it becomes a game of Twenty Questions, because the truth is I'd give anything to give one of those answers. I don't want to stand out or receive any extra attention. I wish I could just say I'm in plastics or software development or something that sounds solid and stoic. Instead, since I don't like to lie or play games, I swallow quickly and murmur that I'm a musician.

Now when most people hear this they will usually think one of three things: (A) you're a loser who plays guitar and takes bong hits in the garage all day while your wife supports you and your family, (B) you're a Christian musical director at the local evangelical church who wears Birkenstocks and sings worship songs about Jesus and the mountain with your eyes closed while your wife supports you and your family, or (C) you're in some horrible third-rate Jimmy Buffett jazz fusion cover band with no chance in hell of ever making it and you're about two seconds away from handing them your fifth attempt at a demo CD to give to anyone they may know in the record business, and your wife supports you and your family. Any way you slice it, it's not good. If it were Bruce Springsteen or Steve Tyler standing in front of them, they wouldn't have to ask. Otherwise they think to themselves, "If you're a musician you're obviously a failure, or I would recognize you, and since I don't, you probably should just give it up because everyone I know has a guitar or banjo or saxophone in the garage or the attic somewhere but they don't call themselves musicians. They dust it off every once in a while and try to remember the three chords they learned in high school, but at some point they have enough sense to hang it up and get a real job."

Most people are nice so they'll repress the urge to smile and walk away to find someone they can better network with, and they'll ask another question or two.

"Oh really, what do you play?" they'll ask politely.

"Well, I'm in a band."

"What kind of music?"

"Well, it's like hard rock or ... punk rock, whatever you wanna call it."

"No shit, really? Hey, honey, this guy's in a punk rock band! Do you guys play local? What's it called?"

"Well, we tour a lot. We're called Pennywise."

"Pennywise? Huh, never heard of it. Carol! Ever heard of Pennywise? No? Wow, that's fantastic. Do you have any records out?"

"Yeah, we've actually put out eight albums."

"Jesus, you've been at it a long time."

"Yep, fifteen years. So what do you do?"

"I'm in plastics. What instrument do you play?"

"Well, I'm the singer."

"The singer? Wow! You don't look like a singer!"

It's funny how often I get this response. It's incredible that people don't see that statement as being completely offensive. When you imagine a lead singer, you think of an incredibly good-looking, charismatic, charming, sexy, hot stud. So saying I don't look like a singer is basically telling me I'm cosmically boring and unattractive. I've often thought that to counteract this I should enter these events wearing a spandex pantsuit with the entire abdomen cut out and holding a microphone screaming, "WHAT'S UP, MEADOWS ELEMENTARY? HOW YOU FEELING?"

So we walk around the classroom and see all the finger-painted rainbows, the Thanksgiving turkeys made by tracing their hands on construction paper, the clay statues of some kind of animal, and the squiggly, crayon line drawings of our family (I'm usually making an angry face and screaming into a microphone). We sit in their little chairs at their little tables and look at all the "See Jane Run" books they are reading, the carpet games they play, and the cubbyholes where they keep their stuff. It's all very nice and quaint and *Little House on the Prairie*-ish, and for some reason I feel slightly embarrassed to be there and can't stop thinking I could still be kept after school for something.

We eventually meet the incredibly sweet and cordial teacher, who has the calm, almost Buddhist-like temperament you'd need to corral thirty raging five-year-olds all day and not go completely postal on them at one point or another. She of course drops the "So what do you do?" bomb right away. I tell her I'm a musician and the name of our band, and I'm amazed and somewhat terrified to find out that she's familiar with our music.

"Don't you have a song on KROQ right now?" Suddenly an ice shard has replaced my spine.

"Um, yes we do.... Oh, doesn't her Thanksgiving turkey look nice. Did she trace her hand to do that?"

"Yes, she did. What's the song called, the one about authority or something?"

"Um, yeah, that's the one.... Oh, honey, look at the drawing of us—she even drew Hamtaro the hamster!"

"Isn't it called 'Fuck Authority'?"

At that moment I realized that this was probably the first time a kindergarten teacher has ever spoken the f-word to a parent on parents' night when she wasn't referring to something their little turd had written on the blackboard, or where the phrase wasn't followed by some kind of psychological freak-out and eventual lawsuit. It was actually used in polite conversation, and it was about me and my song on the radio. I began to feel the parallel layers of the universe collapse in around me.

"Um, yeah. That's the one."

This is when I go into my explanation that everyone in the band writes songs and this is one the guitarist wrote, and he's a certifiable psychopath and has always had problems with authority, and really it's not my favorite song, either, to tell you the truth, and I have no idea why the radio picked that song to play when we really have a lot of songs that are positive and life-affirming and this one really isn't representative of the band and I wish they wouldn't even play that one and "…oh my, look at that clay sculpture! Is that a cow or a hippopotamus?"

This brings up an important subject about being a dad from the punk world. How do you reconcile the "Fuck Authority" attitude that punk rock has always championed when you are trying to teach your kids to respect authority, especially your own? How can I go out every night and sing that song at the top of my lungs and the next time I tell my six-year-old to quit goofing around and go to bed not expect her to come over and flip me the bird and tell me where to cram it because I'm the *Man* and I've been repressing six-year-olds like her for centuries? Shouldn't I be proud at that moment, that is, if I wasn't the world's biggest sell-out hypocrite? If I expect her to follow my rules, shouldn't I preface my introduction to the song each time we play it by saying, "Well, yes, technically, 'Fuck Authority,' but really only when you're old enough and it's appropriate, otherwise you should probably do what you're told or you could be grounded."

PUNK ROCK DAD

I am a punk rock dad. When I drive my kids to school in the morning, we listen to the Ramones, the Clash, or the Descendents and nothing else. They can listen to whatever former Mouseketeer they want to hear chirping out the latest pop hit crafted by a Swedish songwriting team when I'm not around, but when I'm behind the wheel, it's the Ramones, the Clash, or the Descendents, and that's it. I go to all the soccer games, dance rehearsals, and piano recitals like all the other dads, but when I feel the need, I also go to punk shows and run into the slam pit and come home bruised and beaten, but somehow feeling strangely better. While the other dads dye their hair brown to cover the gray, I dye mine blue from time to time. I make their lunches, kiss their boo-boos, and tuck them in at night, and then go in the garage and play Black Flag and Minor Threat songs at criminal volume. I pay my taxes, vote in all presidential and gubernatorial elections, serve jury duty, and reserve the right to believe that most political figures are hopelessly corrupt, that there's a vast right wing conspiracy to screw the working man out of his social security benefits, and that the head of the PTA at school is possibly in on it. The first record I ever bought was *Never Mind the Bollocks, Here's the Sex Pistols*, and I've never owned an Eagles or Led Zeppelin album, but most importantly, I came of age in the late 1970s and early '80s, and took part in the revolution when punk rock tore open the flaccid music scene and altered the cultural landscape the world over. This is what makes me a punk rock dad.

THE BLANK GENERATION

There are millions of other dads out there just like me who grew up in the 1970s. Our first memories of TV were when our favorite episode of *Casper, the Friendly Ghost* was preempted by President Nixon's sweating face resigning after the Watergate scandal. We remember block-long oil embargo gas lines, manic disco dancing, the Iran hostage takeover, and strangely buoyant hairstyles. *Three's Company* and Fleetwood Mac ruled the airwaves.

The political mood was the confusing aftermath of America's loss of innocence with JFK, the Vietnam War, Kent State, and the paranoid factoids in *Time* magazine telling us that our combined nuclear arsenals could blow up the world ten times over. The peace-and-love movement of smoking weed and "lovin' the one you're with" had crashed and burned into the "Me decade" of mutual distrust, mountains of cocaine, and a spiraling divorce rate.

The 1970s became one long valium-addicted hangover from the 1960s, where our parents went into scream therapy with their psychiatrists and decided it was their happiness that mattered most, not their kids', so they split up, and Dad started spending his weekends with his secretary in a condo down in Baja. All of a sudden, we were having two Christmases and two Thanksgivings every year, one in Mexico and another spent decorating the tree and passing the turkey to your mom's new boyfriend, Doug. We became latchkey kids, left home alone in our rooms playing Pong with our Pet Rock and spanking it to our Farrah Fawcett poster while the parents worked two jobs to save up for another vacation in Acapulco for more disco dancing, piña coladas, and wife swapping. We were bored, disenfranchised, and frustrated with everything. Music and TV sucked, as did the whole seemingly hopeless direction of the entire human race.

Punk rock came along at the end of the decade just when we needed it most, and in the chaos of it, everything made perfect sense. The music was fast, furious, and seethed with adolescent resentment and frustration. It was anti-fashion, anti-authority, anti-everything. Verbose social critics saw it as a postmodern expression of Dadaism, an exercise in semiotics, the rejection of traditional cultural values, and the symptom of an underlying societal disease. We saw it as a righteous way to blow off steam and piss off the status quo. We would shove their screwed-up world right back in their faces, wear torn-up clothes, and put a middle finger up to the mainstream. We would never grow up, never sell out, and never give in. We'd change the world with distortion, anarchy, and angst. Just as our parents used Elvis Presley, Jerry Lee Lewis, and the Beatles as the soundtrack to their adolescent rebellion, we would use Johnny Rotten, Keith Morris, and Joey Ramone.

> I don't wanna live, to be thirty seven
> I'm living in hell, is there a heaven?
> Live fast, die young
> Live fast, die young
> Live fast, die young
>
> **—The Circle Jerks**

Music had never been this pissed off before. Up until then, American music had been about the backwoods twang of hillbilly country, Delta Blues, smooth jazz, the jovial bebop of rock 'n' roll, the spaced out sounds of psychedelia, and most nauseatingly, the pilled out lethargy of 1970s FM soft rock, but punk music, almost more than any other musical revolution before it, perfectly captured the bilious spirit of the age. With the cold war, nuclear proliferation, and political corruption rampant, there was a sense at the end of the decade that the human condition had become pointless, plastic, and corrupt. Punk rock emerged as a reaction to a world "falling apart at the rifts" and served to give us a sense of power and identity when we had none. For a few brief years we felt unity and pride in the fact that we had responded to the ruined society we'd inherited from our parents by emphatically rejecting it, and if we had to go down in a nuclear holocaust, we would go down singing a fast, angry punk song and bashing into each other in the slam pit in some bizarre nihilistic, cathartic purge, our song a caterwaul from the blank generation.

What about afterward? Most of the good punk bands broke up, sold out, or imploded. New wave and heavy metal took over where punk rock left off and MTV packaged it and sold it in a medium that was easily digested by the masses. Seemingly overnight, the rage had been extinguished by commerce and complacency. Most of us finished high school and then had to get real jobs. We went to college and training seminars, got the company car, the 401(k), the expense account, and the tiny cubicle with our very own computer. We found a cheap apartment in town somewhere and spent our weekends drinking and smoking at the local bar, wondering what the hell we were doing with our lives.

So how were we to know that one day we'd find our perfect mate in a dingy club or used record store somewhere, and after going through so many one-sided crushes and high-maintenance psycho girlfriends, we thought we'd never find a nice one, so we asked her to marry us just because we felt lucky that anyone would want to hang around with someone who looks, acts, and smells like we do. We got married and soon after were hearing the pitter-patter of little Doc Marten–adorned feet. Then one day, out of nowhere, we have three kids and a minivan, we're going to T-ball games and spending five hours a night trying to put to bed what will not go to bed without a heroic battle. We are pleading with them to eat their peas and carrots because "Goddamn it they can't just eat French fries for every meal," and then we're fist fighting with some other dad at Wal-Mart at eleven o'clock on Christmas Eve over the last Cabbage Patch doll and getting the stomach flu twice a year when our daughter brings it home from basketball camp. Before we knew it, we were unwillingly thrust into a world of boring PTA meetings, psycho Stepford moms, contentious weekend soccer games, and playgrounds teeming with snot-nosed kindergartners. Just when we had successfully rebelled against our parents, we became them.

SOMETHING TO BELIEVE IN

The great news is that after having spent the first half of our lives pissed off and complaining and feeling frustrated all the time, we find that becoming parents can be the one thing that gives our meaningless lives a sense of purpose. It's the most fucked up, difficult, heartbreaking thing in the world to take on, but, apologies to those who don't have kids for whatever reason, it's why we're here. It's part of the deal. Someone gave birth to you and wiped your ass and listened to you whine and cry all day and night, and now you get to do it for someone else so we can procreate this messed up species. Believe in whatever man-made religion, celebrity science-fiction cult, or boogeyman you want to donate ten percent of your life savings to, but having children is one thing we know our species is biologically driven to do; if it wasn't, none of us would be here, simple as that. With overpopulation and the lack of good health care, it's actually great that some people choose not to have kids, but for many of us, it can be the one thing that gives you a shot at true happiness in what can otherwise seem like a cold, forbidding world, and it may even help you begin to finally accept some of the responsibilities you've been actively rebelling against your whole life.

When I first discovered punk rock by purchasing *Never Mind the Bollocks*, I finally felt like I wasn't alone in the universe. Before then I had no idea what my place in the world was—or even who I was. Parents and friends didn't understand me, and most of the time I just felt classically misunderstood and out of step with everyone else. Finding punk rock let me know there were other disillusioned souls out there who had bottled-up resentment and frustrations that could only be purged by distortion and angst. Having kindred spirits in the world helped lessen the anxiety about facing the unknown, and for several years I felt comfort knowing I had a secret brotherhood in the punk rock community, listening to their Black Flag and T.S.O.L. records alone in their bedrooms like I did. This was something to believe in, somewhere to belong.

Decades later when I found out my wife, Jennifer, and I were having our first child, my initial feeling was one of crippling anxiety about us being alone to take on the awesome responsibility of bringing a child into the world. When we put that little jelly-bean-sized infant into our giant car seat to take her home for the first time, and she was so small the strap wouldn't even hold her in and her tiny pea head kept slumping down in the seat, I suddenly thought, "We're not ready for this. We should take her back into the hospital and let the professionals take care of her. I'm a punk rocker, for God's sake! You don't give us babies! We're the most irresponsible people on the planet!"

When I did finally accept that I was a dad and it wasn't all some huge cosmic mistake, I realized I would be entering a world of parenting that can at times seem like it's only populated by every type of conservative religious fanatic/competitive psycho you can imagine, who would, in turn, look at me like I was the freak. So it's good to know that now there are millions of parents out there just like me, who still have the spirit of punk rock in their hearts while they chaperone the kids to ballet class and kindergarten, even though sometimes it feels like we're raising our kids on another planet.

I DON'T WANNA GROW UP

The whole alternative/punk movement can be seen as one child-like refusal to grow up and take on responsibility, and the image of the immature, tattooed, and pierced alternative slacker/stoner, addicted to Internet porn and video games, has become the archetype that defines our entire generation. For me, becoming a parent became the one thing that finally forced me to grow up and accept that I wasn't a kid anymore. It didn't mean I had to turn into a boring old fart bag who sits in a recliner all day and yells at the kids to stay off the grass, but almost everything changes when you become a dad. Just try to stay out all night and then wake up in time to go to your kid's soccer game. A few friends and I went to a Bad Religion show a while back and tried to pretend we were still eighteen by pounding a few beers in the parking lot, swilling multiple rum and Cokes in the V.I.P. area, and then continuing on to the after-party, where we engaged in a shot-drinking contest until the wee hours. When I finally stumbled home, Jennifer informed me that daughter number two had an 8 A.M. soccer game that morning, a few short hours away. Sitting in the fetal position in a lawn chair on the sidelines with my hat pulled down over my sunglasses, I was fooling no one. My voice was thrashed, my complexion two or three shades of sea foam green, and I smelled like the bar I'd nearly passed out in a few hours earlier. Every time I stood up to watch number two take one of a hundred shots on goal, I immediately had to sit back down in fear of adding some of last night's Jägermeister and nachos supreme to the game field. Next time I'll stay home.

My kids are what get me up in the morning, literally and figuratively. I can't really remember the last good night's sleep I've had. Usually it starts with the little one, daughter number three, crying from her crib at about 1 A.M., an hour or so after I've turned off *Letterman*. So instead of carrying her around and bouncing her back to sleep or just letting her cry in the dark and giving her an abandonment complex, I grab her and throw her in our bed. She goes right back to sleep, and I get about two good hours in until about 3 A.M., when the oldest one appears at the side of the bed saying she's had a scary dream about a headless skeleton and wants to sleep in our bed. It doesn't take number two long to figure out she's the only one who's not in mom and dad's bed, so by four o'clock the entire family is in our bed, I'm hanging off the side with someone's elbow lodged in my neck, and I've been kicked in the nuts about five times already. This is a good night's sleep now.

It's kind of like someone warning you when you are about to go on a particularly frightening roller-coaster ride or you're about to watch an extremely scary film. Of course you should go; they just want to warn you that you're probably not really prepared for what you're getting into, so here's a little cautionary advice: "Don't look down on the third loop," and "Avert your eyes during the scene where the severed head pops out of the shipwreck if you're prone to heart failure, but of course you should go!" They went and they're going again because it was frickin' awesome. This is why I have three kids.

STORY OF MY LIFE

I am the world's forgotten boy
The one who's searching to destroy

—Iggy & the Stooges

I didn't choose punk rock. Punk rock chose me. Mainly because the small L.A. beach town where I was raised was destined to become a fertile punk rock breeding ground, but also because a genetic malfunction virtually ensured that when I first heard its forbidden beat, I would respond emphatically. I probably would have been perfectly content to grow up and become a happy-go-lucky, productive member of society, but somehow, while floating around in my mother's fallopian tubes on the journey down to my uterine home, I inherited a mutated gene from one of my ancestors that meant when I came out, instead of having both eyes gazing lovingly up at my parents, they were both staring at my nose, unable to move, as if a fly were resting there that I couldn't stop looking at.

Strabismus is a condition that affects thousands of babies worldwide. It means that somewhere in my fetal development, my eyes decided they didn't want to work together and focus on objects like a team, and instead looked around independent of each other. The wonderful layman's term for this condition is called "being fucking cross-eyed." The problem is that it seems to be one of the few handicaps, along with stuttering and chronic flatulence, that most people have absolutely no problem with making fun of to your face. You walk up to them with one eye staring at your nose and they think you're being funny. Those who are so gifted to be able to mimic the condition will salute you by laughing and doing it right back to you. You wouldn't walk up to a kid with one leg and start hopping around like you're on a pogo stick, but for some reason a person with screwy eyes is fair game.

The first time I realized I had this deformity was a particularly jarring experience for someone of my tender age. My parents must have kept me hidden in a closet until kindergarten or broken all our mirrors because for all I knew I was a happy, well-adjusted youngster, but when I walked out onto the playground for the first time, I met a kid who was running around scaring little girls by yanking his lips apart and moaning like he was Frankenstein. When I approached to join their game, he took one look at me and my eyes and said, "Yeah, you do that, and we'll chase the girls around together." Apparently, my normal visage was enough to horrify five-year-old girls into a panic.

Last time I checked, no five-year-old likes to be singled out as being different from everyone else, so I remember starting to feel a little ashamed and freaked out about my condition as far back as kindergarten. It's hard to win friends and influence people when the first rule is to always look people in the eye. Later on, with surgery, the effect was lessened to the point where instead of staring at my nose, I could look at you with one eye but the other would kind of wander off into orbit like a lost satellite. I'm convinced this mutated gene and the harsh vibes I got from other kids had a profound impact on my later personality. The mind is a wonderful, adaptive thing in our formative years, and since the soul craves acceptance by our peers, I compensated for my ocular malfunction by deciding that if I did weird things and acted strangely to go along with it, people would think I was just being funny. I started being disruptive in class and doing idiotic things to divert attention away from my eye problem. I'd use my hands to make farting noises while the teacher was talking, wear ridiculous fishing hats to school, and eat gross things off the sidewalk for the other kids' amusement—your typical cry-for-help attempts to get people to accept me. Pretty soon I became popular at school just for being a total freak.

My psycho rebelliousness only increased in junior high, and since I had no fear of getting in trouble, I started becoming a regular outside the principal's office after school. One Friday afternoon I convinced a friend that going into my dad's refrigerator in the garage and drinking as much beer as we could stomach before our Little League game was a great idea. I don't remember much of the details of what happened afterward, but I do know it involved me eating a significant amount of dirt in the infield, flipping off my baseball coach, punching a kid on the other team, and culminated in me being chased around the outfield by my sister and her friends while disgusted parents looked on from the bleachers. I remember thinking even before I opened the first beer that I was probably going to get in a lot of trouble for doing this, but that didn't stop me. I did it because I wanted to break up the monotony of everyday life, and getting into trouble seemed like the best way to do it. That memorable Friday evening finally ended with me pulling down my pants and streaking the full length of Ardmore Avenue, ass cheeks to the wind.

Like many other kids I never stopped rebelling, and when punk rock came around it was like we were meant for each other. I remember reading a newspaper article about a new kind of music scene happening in London and seeing pictures of these freaky-looking teenagers with spiked, colored hair, studded leather jackets, and military boots, sulking around and flipping off the camera. It looked really awful and a lot of fun. The band they were writing about was called the Sex Pistols, so that same day I went up to the local Music Plus store and picked up the garish Day-Glo pink and green album which spelled out the title on the cover like a ransom note, *Never Mind the Bollocks, Here's the Sex Pistols!* I had no idea what bollocks were but I brought it home, and from the opening thunderous guitar chord, followed by Johnny Rotten's snotty, antagonistic growl, I was hooked. This was exactly what I had been waiting for.

Rotten sounded like a kid who didn't care what anyone thought of him, his voice being the sonic equivalent of giving the finger to everyone who ever oppressed you in life; your parents, your teachers, the cops, the jock bullies at school, everyone who'd ever made you feel powerless, and for a kid growing accustomed to having people look at him strange because of an eye problem, this attitude of not caring what other people thought suited me perfectly. Hearing the Sex Pistols was like instantly finding out who I was. I was punk. I knew it deep down in my soul. Whether or not I ever had a Mohawk or played in a band didn't matter, this was how I'd always felt inside. It was a reaction to all the rejection I had received since I first walked out on that playground when I was five. "If you won't accept me as I am, then I don't want to be anything like you."

After my initiation into punk music with the Sex Pistols, I started seeking out my new identity anywhere I could find it. The Southern California version of the new musical phenomenon was far different from London's, with its emphasis on fashion and facial piercings, and New York, with its avant-garde art scene mentality; ours was populated by bored, middle-class, angry suburban youths looking for an outlet for their antipathy and frustration. Across the street from one of my best friends lived the O'Connor brothers, two raging street kids a couple years older who lived alone with their mother in a small white clapboard house, and whose daily regimen consisted of surfing at 26th Street, skateboarding the alleys and driveways behind the beach houses, listening to punk rock, and getting into trouble. Thanks to the O'Connor brothers and a cast of other local punks who hung around their house drinking cans of Bud all day, I was given a steady diet of the best music punk rock had to offer. Every day I would come home from school, turn on the crappy Panasonic stereo I confiscated from my parents' living room, and listen to the nihilistic sounds of the Adolescents, T.S.O.L, and the Dead Kennedys, memorizing every word and staring at their album covers for tips on how to look, dress, and act punk. The sound track of my life constantly echoing through my ears as I rode my skateboard through the back alleys and down the steep hills of the South Bay became one of adolescent rage and defiance. I'm not sure what we were all so angry about, probably just overactive hormones and a craving for independence from all the figures of authority continually trying to rein us in.

Maybe it was sheer suburban boredom, but the music matched exactly how I felt.

For no reason other than the fact that I had absolutely no fear of looking stupid in public, during my sophomore year I answered an ad in the local newspaper for a high school band looking for a singer. I had never tried to sing before, or even been told I had a good voice, but I knew I really wanted to scream into a microphone like my punk heroes and let out some of the rage I'd bottled up all those years. The band was three guys from Redondo who were looking to play cover songs at parties. I suggested "Clampdown" by The Clash and "Zero Hour" by The Plimsouls. They learned the songs and I brought over my rented Radio Shack P.A. system to their garage and set it up. The thing howled and screamed feedback during our entire first practice, but after two or three false starts, underneath the earsplitting racket of the too-loud guitar, poorly timed drumming, and my Peter Brady vocals, we started playing something that vaguely resembled an actual song. At one point of particularly impressive sophomore garage band dexterity, we all looked up at each other and smiled. We were a band.

This led to years of backyard party bands, where I'd get ridiculously hammered and make a total ass of myself, but just like in kindergarten, it helped people look past the eye problem and gave me just enough popularity in the high school battlefield that I didn't have to sit in my room alone and grow hair on my palms. The bands I was in played cover songs of whatever people wanted to hear so they could hook up with each other, lock braces, and struggle with bra straps in the backseats of their parents' cars afterward. We'd play punk, party music, and stupid songs I wrote about girlfriends, hating your teachers, and surfing.

After the punk scene had pretty much imploded during the late 1980s, and was taken over by heavy metal boys in tight leather crotchless ass pants, chick hair, and makeup, I gave up on my dreams of rock stardom, went to college, and tried to figure out what I was going to do with my life. While wasting my time at San Diego State, surfing, and getting bounced from frat parties, on the weekends when I'd drive back to the South Bay, I started noticing a group of girls cruising around town in a blue '65 Mustang Fastback, all of them hot, local, blond surf chicks, but the girl driving with the sleepy green eyes seemed different from your typical Brian Wilson surfer girl. She had a certain soulful quality about her, without the fake, valley girl, airhead mentality some of the local girls had adopted to make themselves seem easily available. Every time I saw her drive by I'd think to myself that was the girl for me, that somehow we were destined to be together, but she just didn't know it yet.

We were finally introduced by some mutual friends at a party and ended up walking down to a park and sat around talking until the sprinklers came on and we ran into a cement tube on the playground, where we fell asleep together. I couldn't have known it then but there was also another more subliminal reason I was attracted to her. She was smart, wryly funny, and beautiful, but also very straight and responsible. At the time we met, my life could have gone two very different ways. I could have continued partying, met some equally self-destructive punk rock girl, and spent my life in rehabs, jail cells, or worse, but meeting her made me want to clean up my act and try to make something of myself. When she was at UC Santa Barbara in college, her roommates called her "Mom" because she was always telling them to be careful, and making sure no one drove drunk, and baking cakes for people's birthdays, and hemming dresses for them. She basically had all the maternal instincts she needed already in place before we ever had kids. Her friends now are always asking her for advice when it comes to dealing with fevers and flus and their children's various rashes and illnesses because they know my wife has read every parenting book out there and is a walking childcare encyclopedia. This couldn't have worked out better for me, being a hedonistic weekend warrior, since she's always keeping me grounded and knows just how far to let me go before I need to be lassoed and reeled back in. It also worked out better for our future family since I'm clueless and know next to nothing about raising kids beyond the fact that you're supposed to hand them five bucks when they ask for it. If we were Sid and Nancy, things would not have worked out as well for us.

With her as my motivation, I eventually started getting better grades and was able to transfer to UCLA and earn a degree in English, putting it to fine use when my dad landed me a job after graduation as an outside sales rep in the air cargo industry. I put on the suit and tie, got the company car, the 401(k), my very own cubicle and computer, and joined the working world. This was right about when I started hearing that my neighbor Jason, from a street over, had started a band called Pennywise.

Jason Thirsk lived next door to my best friend who used to bully him and his little brother Justin. I always liked Jason because instead of picking on his little brother like most older siblings, he always stood up for him. Later on, he grew up to be a guy everyone in the South Bay liked and admired. He had a standard uniform he wore every day of long shorts, a wrinkled T-shirt, and black Doc Martens. He always had an emphatic celebratory nickname he'd greet you with whenever you walked up to him, with mine being one of the most complicated. He called me "Jim-Bo-Billy-Bob Omar Sharif." I have no idea how he came up with that, but I loved hearing it every time I saw him. He listened to all kinds of punk music, could answer any TV trivia question, especially those concerning his beloved *Bonanza*, and all the girls loved him unconditionally. He was just one of those all-around likable guys, the kind I could never be, which was why I liked him so much.

Pennywise had been playing together for just under a year when Fletcher, the 6'5", 300-pound guitar player, came into the local watering hole where I was playing in a cover band and told me they needed a new lead singer. I went over to their practice place, which was a small, beat-down, one-car clapboard garage covered in skate punk graffiti. The windows buzzed and the whole place rattled and shook from the sound of them playing inside. I remember standing outside the door listening and wondering if I should go in. I was about to walk away when I thought to myself that I'd never worried about looking stupid before, so I might as well give it a try. It was impossible for me to know at the time that when I opened the door to that sweaty carpet cave, I was opening the door to the next twenty years of my life.

After that first practice on Irena Street, with Fletcher playing as fast and as loud as he could, Byron, the drummer, doing tom rolls up and down his kit in the time it would take most drummers to do one, Jason sweating and hammering away on his beloved Rickenbacker bass, and me just trying to keep up with them, things started to develop pretty fast for us. We played a lot of backyard parties that got bigger and rowdier each time, usually ending with a battalion of cop cars swooping in and scattering the crowd. With the help of a local friend who was starting his own label, we made our first recording at a tiny studio in Venice Beach, where we were constantly being told by the engineers to quit screwing around and play the songs right. A DJ at a local college station gave it to Brett Gurewitz, the renowned punk-scene guitarist and songwriter for Bad Religion, who had just put out our favorite new album, *Suffer*, on Epitaph Records, a tiny label he'd started on a loan from his dad. Fortunately for us, Brett liked what he heard and signed us to a record deal based on a cassette tape we made of our new songs on a ghetto blaster. I can still remember when Fletcher and Jason came to my house to tell me we were getting signed by Epitaph. We whooped it up and then sat there in disbelief that someone was going to give four screwed-up, delinquent kids from the South Bay a chance to record our own album.

Even though we had been signed to a record deal I still had to keep my day job, and it soon became apparent that I hadn't inherited my father's talent for salesmanship, as I hadn't landed a single account in three months. I quit that job, and while moonlighting as a punk singer, I found work at an advertising brokerage firm, booking TV commercials to air during episodes of *Baywatch* and *Jeopardy!* At night we were recording our first album in a small one-bedroom bungalow in Hollywood and playing shows in dingy Sunset Strip clubs like Coconut Teaser and the Anti-Club, where local punk gangs from L.A., Venice, and the Valley would use our shows as a battleground for bloody gang fights. I'd go to work in the morning and tell my boss about how the night before I'd been surrounded in the bathroom and nearly stabbed by gang members, and he would just shake his head and complain to the team manager every time I mistakenly keyed in an ad to air during the wrong TV program that he had "a punk rocker for an assistant."

Eventually, I convinced Jennifer that we should get married, and we moved into a tiny apartment in Hermosa. After two more equally unsuccessful jobs in the advertising industry, and with her supporting us as a sales team manager at a software company, I quit my day job so I could go on tour and gamble on a future as a full-time singer in a punk band. For a bunch of beach kids raised on beer and fast music, being let loose on the world in the back of a converted Dodge van to go on tour meant that we would basically start partying when we left for the first show, and wouldn't stop until we got home a month later. It's not hard to see how, with hours of sitting around all day waiting to play later that night, the band and crew of a four-band bill would have little left to do but drink copious amounts of alcohol and challenge one another to perform ridiculous punk rock stunts, of which Fletcher was the grand champion, performing his patented up-the-nose and out-the-mouth chain trick that would cause him to throw up on unsuspecting bystanders. Our record deal gave us carte blanche to continue acting like young, irresponsible punks, and even though our songs were Minor Threat- and 7 Seconds-inspired Thoreau-ian punk rock rallying cries to "live life by your own rules," when we were on the road it was all about chaos and destruction.

With Fletcher as our ring leader, he and his band of merry drunken crew men would destroy backstage areas and antagonize security guards and local authorities and basically anyone trying to rope in his good time. During our show the crowd would sometimes spontaneously come up on stage unprovoked, breaking down the wall between band and audience, a spectacle that usually ended in something that to the untrained eye would look like a small-scale riot, but what was really just a bacchanalian celebration of being alive and having a good time. Afterward Fletcher would adopt a group of fans, maybe destroy a minimart or truck stop while stocking up on beer and microwaveable burritos, and then go back to the hotel to trash more rooms and hassle security guards. We'd get a few hours of sleep and then wake up to do it all again.

While the punk rock, surf, and skate scene fell on lean times in the late 1980s, a strong resurgence began to develop in the early '90s when Nirvana exploded, and action sports aerialists Kelly Slater and Tony Hawk started pushing their sports to new levels. When young video directors started using music from underground skate punk bands like us, NOFX, Rancid, the Offspring, and Blink 182 as the sound tracks to their videos, we saw our popularity increase around the world. By our second tour we were playing to large crowds of surfers, skaters, and street punks all over Europe, Australia, and North America, anywhere there was a healthy independent music scene happening. All the surf industry companies wanted us wearing their clothes and sporting their shades, and where we came from, being sponsored meant you'd made it, so who were we to turn them down? I can remember being on stage at one particularly massive festival in Europe and glancing over at Jason, and we exchanged a look of amazement, that somehow, against all odds, we were living out our dreams of playing music for thousands of people, and every night seemed like a nonstop party.

With Jennifer at home moving up the corporate ladder at her new job, we planned that one day when we were ready, we'd settle down and start a family, but at the time I was having too much fun being young and carefree and traveling the world playing in my punk band and watching Fletcher barf on people. The threat of any kind of real responsibility seemed decades away.

PARTY AT GROUND ZERO

I was furiously playing guitar in our sweltering garage one summer afternoon trying to come up with the fiftieth song for our next album and getting nowhere. I'd been working on one song all afternoon, thinking I'd just come up with the next big feel-good punk rock hit of the summer, when I realized it was "Sweet Home Alabama," just played a lot faster. I was staring at the six strings of my Les Paul, waiting for inspiration, when suddenly the garage door swung open, blinding me. Jennifer knows not to interrupt the songwriting genius when he's working, so already I wasn't in a great mood. She then came over and gave me what looked like a birthday card in a yellow envelope.

The first wave of panic hit me because I thought I must have forgotten our anniversary. I quickly started looking around the garage at the hammers and wrenches on the pegboard so I could fashion a makeshift present to give to her, but this was the summer and our anniversary was in May. I can always remember this because we were married during the weekend of the L.A. Riots in '92, up on a hill in Palos Verdes that overlooks the city. (For our first dance, our guests got to watch the smoke rising from the burning Korean grocery stores behind us.) I opened the envelope, took out the card, and read on the cover, "To the new father-to-be... "

Some guys react to the news that they're going to be a father like someone has just thrown a toaster into their bathtub. They're in such denial they get all pissed off and want to know how it happened, as if they weren't in the same room when she was riding them bareback like a mechanical bull for eight hours. Others who'd been planning to get their wives pregnant are just relieved to find out that all their plumbing works. There's something that makes guys want to trade high fives and moon walk and salute the crowd like they've just sunk the game-winning shot when they find out they've impregnated their wives, when in fact all they did was climb on top and poke their girlfriend for the hundredth time.

Although we'd been planning on having kids one day, it always seemed like something way off in the distant future. When she first told me she was going off the pill, I must have processed it like everything else in the daily list of chores she gives me while I'm drinking my coffee and reading the morning paper; in other words, it went in one ear and out the other. "I need you to take some shirts to the dry cleaners, stop and get a quart of milk, I went off the pill so we could be having kids soon and your life could be over, and, oh yeah, don't forget to pay the phone bill."

The news hit me like a sucker punch to the gut. Staring down at the card, I got a hot flash and my knees started to buckle a little bit. I wasn't ready for this. I'm the singer for a punk band; you don't give us babies. You give us a microphone and a can of beer, put us in the back of a van, and send us on the road for the rest of our lives. I don't change diapers, I yell out in defiance and rage against machines. Our band was just about to go on the Warped Tour and I was staring down a month's worth of shows in the heat of the summer, playing to thousands of sweaty, shirtless, adrenaline-pumped dudes, and I didn't have time for morning sickness and Lamaze class and baby-proofing, much less children. Besides, I was the most irresponsible person I knew. In high school I'd been suspended three times and expelled once. I eventually graduated from college but that was only because they had the best parties there. I'd had a total of four jobs since graduating and ended up quitting all of them within a year, and now I spent most of my time going on stage and acting like a spoiled three-year-old, complaining about how the world wasn't exactly how I liked it. I was not the picture of a perfect responsible dad in training, I was a world-class screwup.

She then showed me the small in-home early pregnancy test and explained many times in detail, to which I again asked multiple times for clarification that the two blue lines meant she was indeed pregnant and that we would be having a baby in nine months time. My mind started racing, thinking about everything that was riding on the backs of those two thin lines, the crushing reality of the decades of responsibility that lay ahead of us, and what it all meant. After all, we both still felt like kids ourselves. Wasn't it just a few years ago we were still in high school, drinking and partying every night, going out to Hollywood to see Social Distortion and X shows, and sponging off our parents for everything we needed in life? Would I still be able to do all the irresponsible, inappropriate, and unseemly things I enjoyed doing? Would I turn Republican? What the hell was going to happen to me? Like two boundaries between our old life and the one that awaited us, as stark and defiant as the border lines that divide countries and states, that tiny pair of indigo streaks defined the edge of a new frontier, bisecting our lives into two strict portions, the years spent before and those spent after having kids.

START SPREADING THE NEWS

After we both digested the results of the E.P.T. and the next day the doctor confirmed that yes, we would be having a baby in nine months time, of course the first thing we wanted to do was start telling people, beginning with my mom and dad. Most parents will be overjoyed and freak out and cry and make a big spectacle of themselves, and you should count yourselves lucky if this happens to you because it pretty much guarantees you're going to have unlimited babysitting for as long as you need it. My parents, on the other hand, had just been through the wonderful, rewarding hell ride of raising my sister and me and probably felt lucky to have made it out the other side relatively sane and with a few dollars left in their savings account. During my junior year of high school on a school night, my mom caught me trying to drunkenly sneak back into my room at five in the morning after being out all night at a show in Hollywood. Since the heavily eye-linered Mike Ness, lead singer of Social Distortion was my latest role model, I'd dyed my hair jet black and used egg whites to make it stand straight up on end, and I had black goth eye makeup streaming down my face. When she came into my room to check on me, instead of having her little cherubic angel tucked in bed for school the next day, she found some kind of prepubescent, postapocalyptic, teenage zombie boy with porcupine hair, laughing drunk and hanging halfway out the window. She took one look at me and yelled, "I'VE RAISED A COUPLE OF FREAKS!" and burst out crying.

So although they were cautiously happy about our big announcement, they both knew all too well what we were getting ourselves into. They probably weren't thrilled to be prematurely forced into the title of grandparents again, either. When they heard the news, I'm sure they had visions of themselves hunched over walkers in polyester tracksuits, ordering the fish sticks and Jell-O plate from the Silver Fox menu at Denny's. They may also have suddenly realized that after having finally pawned me off onto society and turned my bedroom into a fitness center, now they'd have more grandchildren to deal with and worry about. So, considering what I'd put them through, I let my mom call herself "Nana" and tried not to be upset when my dad didn't use the "World's Best Grandpa" beer holder I gave him right away.

When it comes to telling your friends, there's a pecking order you need to follow because if your pretty good friend finds out before your best friend, your best friend will be pissed. If this person hears that you're having a kid from the guy at the local skateboard shop, he might not say anything, but inside, you're dead to him. Our friends who already had kids were happy for us, because now they had someone to swap diaper stories with, but we could tell that some of the others weren't as thrilled with the news. Our graduation into parenthood forced some of them to unwillingly take stock of their own lives, especially those that had the kind of parents who were constantly asking them when they were going to get married and give them some grandchildren. Some of my friends probably worried that they were losing a drinking buddy to a life of dirty diapers, parenting groups, and playgrounds. To them, I may as well have said we were moving to Alaska, because even with promises that we would write, they knew they'd be lucky to see us at all between birthday parties, Disneyland trips, and piano recitals.

I'm not sure how my fellow bandmates took the news, either, because, let's face it, being a dad isn't very punk rock. Punk is supposed to be about nihilism, and nihilism and parenting don't really go hand in hand. Becoming a father means that you actually have to care about something and begin to take on responsibility, whereas punk rock is about not giving a crap about anything. I'm sure they worried about how I was going to maintain my punk rock attitude while pushing around a baby stroller and carrying a diaper bag. They also probably feared that this development was going to put some pretty strict limitations on the amount of time I'd be able to go on tour if I needed to be at home spooning bites of mushed carrots into a baby's mouth. Although no one let on, I'm sure they were wondering if my becoming a father would make me lose my edge. What would it do to our tough guy image if I was doing stage dives with a one-year-old in Winnie the Pooh pajamas?

I tried not to let anyone's reaction to the news that we were having a kid get to me though, especially the ones who heard the news, shrugged, and asked me to pass the beer nuts. This was my deal and I couldn't control what other people thought about it. I just tried to follow the golden rule: "Do unto others how you'd want them to do unto you, and if they still have a problem, screw 'em." For your buddy who's worried that he's going to lose his wingman, you take him out for a cold beer and explain that the "new" you is going to be the same as the "old" you, except the "new" you might have a baby strapped to his chest and spit-up running down his shoulder. If he still complains, you buy him a soft taco and tell him to quit being a wuss.

NAUSEA

When it came to pregnancy, I knew next to nothing about what to expect other than what I'd seen on TV shows. I had sitcom images of my wife turning into some kind of swollen hormonal bitch from hell, throwing up like a lawn sprinkler after eating pickles and ice cream all day, and looking like she'd swallowed a beach ball. I found out soon enough that physical signs of pregnancy are different for most women. Some go through the entire pregnancy like one of those long-distance runners who look as happy and energetic crossing the finish line as they did at the start, while others look like the one who collapsed halfway through and crapped her running shorts. The wife of one of my best friends pretty much puked all the time. You could be sitting there talking to her and just mention the words "pepperoni pizza" or "baloney sandwich" and she would just quietly open her purse and hurl into it. Jennifer didn't throw up that much, but she was tired, achy, and felt vaguely nauseous the entire first trimester. She was also so absentminded she'd miss doctors' appointments, lose her car keys, and then get all flustered and just take a nap somewhere.

Two symptoms Jennifer did experience were random food cravings and a heightened sense of taste and smell. She could smell someone opening a can of tuna in another area code and would promptly begin to dry heave. There were times when we would be watching a TV commercial and all of a sudden she'd become ravenous for Chinese chicken salad or a pint of cookie dough ice cream. I tried not to argue or complain when late at night she needed me to get out of bed, put on my clothes, and drive to Taco Bell for a bean and cheese burrito with sour cream, giving me specific instructions for there to be no onions whatsoever, because "if I see or smell onions, or even if I think about the smell of onions too long, I'm going to barf." I tried to see these opportunities as a way to earn some husband-of-the-year brownie points, which I could cash in at a later date, and if I added to my gut a little, people might think I was having a sympathy pregnancy and say what a sweet guy I was for doing that.

Apparently some of the other physical signs that pregnancy can include but not be limited to are leg cramps, back pain, constipation, hemorrhoids, sore and engorged breasts, swollen ankles, skin rashes, itching, head and body aches, a constant need to pee, vaginal discharge, frequent vivid dreams, water retention and bloating, gas, bleeding gums, hot flashes, spider veins, general overall shortness of breath, and fatigue. Pregnant women also get to worry about the wonderful things that can happen after delivery, such as stretch marks, saggy deflated boobs, and whether or not their cooch will ever return to its former elasticity after it's been stretched out like one of those African tribeswomen who cram dinner plates into their lips. Because Jennifer had to suffer through all the glamorous symptoms and debilitating anxieties of pregnancy that I got to sail through like a vacation in the

Caribbean, it wasn't surprising that at times she could seem a little moody.

I'd heard all the horror stories that, for some guys, pregnancy can seem like one long nine-month PMS party. The term "emotional roller coaster" had to have been coined by an expectant father gamely trying to negotiate the twists, turns, and backward loops of pregnancy, and probably by a guy who'd just had an ashtray thrown at his head by a woman surrounded by boxes of Kleenex and chocolate-covered macadamia nuts. Lucky for me, my wife was just so happy that she was about to become the mom she'd always wanted to be that she didn't have a lot of glass-shattering freak-outs or emotional meltdowns. She spent most of her time reading child care and parenting books and getting ready for the big day. There were a few times, however, when I'd be sitting on the couch minding my own business and all of a sudden she'd be incredibly pissed off, saying that I'd forgotten to take out the trash again and now the whole house wreaked and that I was a lazy bastard. I tried not to tell her it was just her hormones talking, because not only is this the last thing she wanted to hear, but the truth was, I had been a lazy bastard and I did forget to take out the trash. Overall, she just wanted a little extra encouragement and help getting up out of chairs and the occasional reassurance that she still looked great and that I wasn't going to leave her now that she looked like a giant bowling ball in stretch pants.

SEX

The other way hormones affected Jennifer was by messing with her libido, and indirectly mine as well. At varying points in the pregnancy, she would want nothing to do with me, and then all of a sudden she'd turn into a rabid porn star. I wouldn't have gotten any for weeks because she wasn't in the mood for it when she was feeling nauseous and fatigued all the time, and then I'd wake up one morning to what felt like my wife holding on to a Butterball turkey bouncing up and down on me. For most guys, late-term coitus can be kind of disconcerting. In the last few months of pregnancy, she would be raring to go, but all I could think about was that my future child was in there a few inches away from the action, and something felt vaguely…well, *wrong* about that. I tried to remember that in a few weeks I'd be getting less than no hanky-panky for a long time and I should probably stock up now, even if it did feel like I was being romantic with a large, warm watermelon.

GOING TO THE OBSTETRICIAN

My first official duty as a punk rock dad was going along with my wife to the initial OB/GYN appointments. These short visits to the female anatomy doctor felt like they lasted a lifetime because everything is painted a pale pink color and there are pictures of flowers everywhere and I always felt a little queasy just being there. I was usually the lone persecuted male in the waiting room surrounded by violently pregnant and vaginally troubled women, who I imagined looked at men like me as the source of all their suffering. It's a little disconcerting for a guy to be in a place where he's surrounded by six-foot-tall diagrams of gaping vaginas and three-dimensional, full-scale plastic models of a uterus sitting next to you on the coffee table among the scattered *Woman's World* magazines. You're always thinking you could turn a corner and walk by a room with an open door and see the old lady from your block spread-eagle on an examination table and pass out and wake up with retrograde amnesia.

Although most of the doctors I've dealt with in my life have been very nice and personable, it's hard for me not to think they all see us as walking sets of symptoms and diagnoses. I'm not Jim, the nice musician guy with three daughters, I'm strabismus and psoriasis with hay fever, terrible family heart history, and acid reflux. They're just taking notes to see how similar my symptoms are to the last thirty people they treated and if my case is just peculiar enough to get a "poor bastard" chuckle during the next round of golf with the other doctors.

The wife and I have a rough time going to the doctor's office in general because we've watched one too many investigative reports on television where a patient goes into the hospital with a nagging cough and somehow contracts a level-10 staph infection and gets the wrong leg amputated, so now we're both paranoid germ freaks. Whenever we step into the doctor's waiting room, we treat it like we've been dropped off at lepers' island and wear enough clothing for an arctic expedition just so no airborne particles of flesh-eating virus or mad cow disease inadvertently land on any exposed skin. I open the door with my sleeve over my hand and pick up the pen for the sign-in sheet the same way, eliciting disdainful looks from the nursing staff. We both try not to breathe at all in the waiting room and don't even look at other patients for fear of getting some kind of black plague spread through casual eye contact.

Even though I'm an incredible germ freak, once I get into the examination room I can't help digging around in there and trying out all the equipment, opening drawers, and seeing what types of forceps and lobotomy tools might be laying around. I also can't stop myself from opening the hazardous waste bin with the bright red "Danger" trash bag liner, just to see if there are any aborted fetuses or Siamese twin halves in there trying to get out. With this type of neurosis going on during our trips to the doctor, it's no wonder we're concerned with what horrors awaited us at the OB/GYN's office.

Lucky for us, we couldn't have asked for a better first obstetrician for a couple as freaked out about childbirth as we were. She was a small Indian woman who must have been a reincarnation of some kind of midwife for the baby Buddha, because she knew every possible detail about childbirth and delivered the answers to our long volleys of paranoid questions with incredible patience and care. My wife could be asking what would happen if the baby comes out and its face is inside out, and the doctor would calmly answer that this rarely happens and it was nothing to worry about and that everything would be fine. She just sat there patiently and waited for our next stupid question, knowing that the only thing that would calm our frayed nerves would be if she answered all our increasingly inane inquiries as if they were all completely valid.

Our second obstetrician was kind of kooky and jaded with the tired look of someone who'd stared down at one too many poorly coiffed vaginas. She was one of the few people who didn't begrudge me when I came in unshowered and disheveled wearing my Black Flag T-shirt with the Pettibone drawing of a raised middle finger. She was the most laissez-faire doc I've ever met, almost as if she'd delivered so many babies and experienced so many different types of childbirths she wouldn't be surprised at all if your baby came out with a full beard in a white suit singing Bee Gees' songs. She'd seen everything twice, and nothing fazed her. We again had a thousand silly questions to which she would just kind of shrug, as if to say, "Well, if that happens, I'll get a turkey sandwich for lunch instead of soup, for all the difference it will make to me." Her relaxed bedside manner again eased our paranoia, which was probably her plan all along.

The most important visit for me to be present for was the ultrasound, where they used a magic wand to electronically produce pictures on a monitor of what was happening inside my wife's womb. This gave us the chance to see the coarse, wavering, gray image that was supposed to be our baby, but to me looked like a black-and-white, badly photocopied map of the world, with our baby looking something like Russia or China. I just pretended I saw what they saw. "Oh, that small, white, circular shape is her leg? Well, she definitely isn't going to be a basketball player! Oh, look, honey, she has your eyes. I've always said your eyes look like two grainy bulbous slits."

Another purpose for the ultrasound, besides confusing me into thinking we were giving birth to some kind of Rorschach test, was that this was when they checked to find out if we were having a boy or a girl, our own little Deborah Harry or Dee Dee Ramone. We wanted to find out in advance just so we'd know what color to paint the baby's room and what kind of clothes to buy and also to save ourselves from any type of unexpected spontaneous response in the delivery room if we didn't get what we were secretly hoping for. I didn't want the kid to come out and have the first words it hears be, "Oh, crap!"

Mainly I was just relieved to find out that the developing fetus had all its limbs in the right places and didn't have devil horns coming out of its head. So when they told us it looked like it was a girl, it hardly seemed to make a difference, as long as everything was normal. Some guys with masculine insecurity issues think that unless they have a boy, the other guys are going to think they are less of a man and make fun of them, and they're too dumb to realize that having these insecurities actually proves the point. Men have millions of X and Y sperm running around in their nut sacks, and it's all one big cosmic spin of the gender roulette wheel what you're going to get. If only macho guys had boys, then the planet would look like one giant gay bar in West Hollywood. I think being happy with the fact that you have a healthy kid proves you're a man, and being depressed and sulking if you don't get a boy makes you a crybaby. This, of course, is coming from a guy with three daughters.

When I accompanied Jennifer to her prenatal visits it showed the world that even though I was a punk rock sociopath, I intended to do the right thing and be involved in the pregnancy, but sometimes seeing my wife spread-eagle on the examination table with the doc sitting between her legs like a mechanic checking under the hood of an old Ford did freak me out. It's kind of like if you were having a rectal exam and the doc was two fingers deep in the place where no person you're not otherwise romantically involved with should ever have their two fingers, and you looked over and saw your wife sitting there smirking at you. You'd feel a little self-conscious too, unless of course you're into that kind of thing. I wanted to stay involved, but not so curious that the doctor had to move me aside just to check my wife's cervix. I was happy to sit several feet away in a chair by the door, next to the giant labia sculpture in the corner.

TOO MUCH PARANOIA

So we'd shared the news with our friends and family and survived the first few trips to the obstetrician, and Jennifer and I would be sitting in our tiny apartment on the couch just trying to get used to the idea that soon we would have a little kid there in between us, our own tiny little helpless creature who looks just like us, eats strained peas, poops, says cute things, and loves us unconditionally, and who would be relying on us to provide everything it needed in life. This was right about when the gargantuan shadow of anxiety came in and began to hover over us day and night. Before, I was always pretty lighthearted and tried not to take things too seriously in life, but I found myself becoming more and more concerned with how this parenthood thing was going to affect my previously irresponsible, independent, punk rock lifestyle.

Many guys from the punk generation have some pretty large issues with their dads, some repressed and unspoken, while others might be right there on the surface, holding a Bud tall and telling you what a loser you turned out to be. If you were one of the lucky ones, he was a great guy, and you and he tossed the ball around in the backyard every day when he came home from work and had great father-son chats in a canoe out on a placid lake somewhere. Chances might be a little better that he was either a patently abusive alcoholic or absent altogether, both physically and emotionally. You can never tell if you're going to get a dad like Ward Cleaver or one who pinches your girlfriend's ass and steals your pot.

So right away, I was a little concerned with what type of father I'd turn out to be. During my childhood I'd caused the untimely death of more than my fair share of hamsters and goldfish due to neglect, and I wondered if I might be constantly having to ask myself if I'd remembered to feed the kids that day. What kind of a role model would I be for my kids when I usually woke up every Monday morning feeling guilty and ashamed about what an ass I'd made of myself over the weekend? I still acted like an overgrown kid myself, eating Fruit Loops for breakfast and watching cartoons, and I still thought arm farts were funny. Would I be able to teach my kids right from wrong, especially since I barely knew the difference myself, and regularly chose the wrong side when I did? What about when they asked me about the birds and the bees? Are you allowed to just rent them a porno and let them figure it out for themselves? Wasn't there a rule book for this type of thing?

I was also concerned about what type of world I was bringing my kid into. We live in Southern California, a half an hour southwest of Hollywood, home to the most superficial, looks-obsessed, artificial, shallow population on the planet, where if you have one microscopic flaw or blemish on your face, you immediately rush to your plastic surgeon and have it lasered, Botoxed, and eviscerated, until everyone on the street looks like a living version of a stretched-out Barbie or Ken doll. There's no way anyone with my DNA would be able to compete in this environment. Would my kid be able to hone and perfect a carefully cultivated "Screw the World" attitude defense mechanism like I had, just to deal with the constant scrutiny of the Tinseltown fashion police?

MONEY WORRIES

The next big cause for concern was, of course, money. Kids aren't cheap. There are clothes to buy, which they'll grow out of in a month, food to purchase that they'll eat two bites of and refuse, medical bills for the six thousand different colds and viruses they'll collect at the germ pool of a school you're paying for them to attend, not to mention the thousands of Christmas and birthday presents that seem to multiply exponentially in cost every year. There's also the skyrocketing cost of sending them to college, where they will take headstand beer bongs and wildly fornicate with other kids from around the country and contract STDs, and then if you're lucky like me, you'll have three fancy weddings to pay for. When I started to add up what it was going to cost to raise a kid, I couldn't pretend I could retire at forty anymore by selling some of my vinyl on eBay.

Now that I was a wholly unprofessional professional musician, the money stress came when I realized being the singer of a punk rock band didn't provide me with the most stable future financially. Record labels don't give you 401(k)s or health insurance plans or stock options, so I always had to worry about how far into the future our record sales would dry up and people would stop coming to our shows, and our record label and agents, so happy to make money off of us during the high points of our career, would unceremoniously kick us to the curb. Would we be able to rock on into our sixties and tour the country as a nostalgia act, so all the aging punkers could get together and bash around the slam pit in their walkers and wheelchairs, or would the next electronic techno music fad take over and push the punk scene unwillingly into obscurity? Like any other working-stiff dad, wondering if he might find a pink slip on his desk on Monday morning, my job security was another thing I worried about late at night, staring wide-eyed at the ceiling and gripping the sheets like death until dawn.

Also in the back of my mind was how I was going to clean up my shamefully unhealthy lifestyle. Throughout the 1980s and most of the '90s, my diet had consisted mainly of fast food, donuts, fluorescent orange chips, instant macaroni and cheese, and microwaveable burritos. I'd head out to a show at night and drink as many rum and Cokes as I could hold down, and then finish it all up by hitting Oki Dog for an enormous chili cheese dog burrito for a midnight snack. When we started going on tour we would have nothing but pizza and beer for dinner every night for a month. I'd never jog or work out, thinking a few laps around the mosh pit or a brisk walk to the cigarette machine would give me all the exercise I needed, and that going to the gym was for yuppies.

I started smoking when I was about eighteen, confusing it for something only incredibly cool people did. Now that I was about to have kids, I didn't want them coming out with a third eye asking for a pack of Camel Lights. I also didn't want to help them along to a life of bronchitis by chain-smoking next to the crib or to have to be trailing around a ventilator to their little league games. Although the punk rock lifestyle has always championed a steady diet of beer and cigarettes, and I'll always crave one more nice long satisfying drag from a menthol 100, apparently emphysema is like being suffocated very slowly over a ten-year period. Cirrhosis of the liver isn't that fun last time I checked, either. "Live Fast, Die Young" is a great song but not as fun in practice. As rewarding as it was to eat, drink, and smoke whatever I wanted, I didn't want my kids spending their teen years visiting me in the cardiopulmonary ward of the local hospice, and I worried that if I didn't clean up my act soon, in nine months we'd be giving birth to the Toxic Avenger.

So with all this dysfunction in my past and the economic needs of raising a kid, I started wondering if I'd be up to the challenge. Yes, I would be, I decided. There wasn't really a choice unfortunately. I'd have to become superdad. I'd work hard, be involved in my kids' upbringing, and deliver beat downs to anyone who looked crossly at them. I would go on tour, play shows, and then come home and tuck the kids into bed at night and clear the monsters from their closets. I needed to go into warrior mode. Armed with the love and trust of my devoted wife, and a few cases of baby wipes, I'd be able to get through anything. I'd teach my kids to be upstanding little warriors of their own, but ones who listen to Iggy Pop and read Nietzsche and Voltaire. It won't be easy, but dads have been succeeding at it for years, and for some reason keep doing it with alarming frequency, so it couldn't be all bad. The kids might hate me from age ten on, no matter what I do, but one day they might have kids of their own and realize what a hero I was. Either that or they'll wait to find out what I plan on leaving them in my will, and if I haven't spent it all on college tuition, new bicycles, and therapy, maybe then they'd finally appreciate me.

STORY OF MY LIFE PART 2

The year that I found out I was going to be a dad for the first time turned out to be the most tumultuous of my entire life. Two of the small underground bands we'd played shows with for years, Green Day and The Offspring, suddenly blew up and started selling millions of albums. Our insular little underground punk scene was the subject of magazine cover articles about "The Year

Punk Broke," and all of a sudden we were all put under music media industry scrutiny we never asked for. We had started out as a small punk band with no plans for the future other than to play to a few friends at backyard keg parties, and now there were record labels and agents expecting us to sell millions of albums. There was also the pressure from our fans and critics from the punk scene not to sell out. For our part, we just wanted to play music and have a good time. We went into the studio and recorded a new album, wondering where the hell this was all going to take us.

After our third album was released and we were beginning to settle into a routine of writing albums and recording and touring, amid the newly expanding independent punk scene, we started noticing that Jason was having more trouble shutting the party down when the tour was over. Coming from a one-square-mile party town that drinks more Budweiser per capita than most small countries, it was hard for us to notice when one of us was developing a problem. When Jason did finally agree that he needed to get some help dealing with it, he called me and said he was glad he'd made the decision to go in for treatment and that the people there had convinced him that he wouldn't live long if he went back to drinking like he had been. He was anxious to get back to writing songs and touring with the band, and I never heard him sound happier.

The problem was that none of us in the band were A.A. counselors and didn't know how to deal with his problem, and going right back on the road with everyone drinking and partying every night turned out to be the last place Jason should be. It wasn't long after our first tour out that he fell back into his old ways. It was incredibly hard for us to understand because he was such a fun-loving guy, no one wanted to bring down his good time, but since we were worried about his health, we decided that he'd have to either agree to quit drinking again for his own good, or go home and deal with the problem. We all thought we were doing the right thing for him. The next day he packed his bags and a cab picked him up and took him to the airport.

We got our friend Randy to fill in for him on bass and went out on the Warped Tour for the first time, hoping Jason would get the help he needed. I'd figured when he was ready he would rejoin the band, and we'd move Randy over to second guitar and everything would be back to normal. We'd never been doing better: The punk scene was alive and vibrant again with more and more bands popping up every day, and I was looking forward to having a kid soon and starting a family of my own. Everything was looking up.

We were out on the road on the Warped Tour one night when I decided I'd better call Jason and check in with him and let him know that as soon as he felt ready, he should come back out on the road with us and start writing songs again. Then we'd be back touring and having a great time just like always. It was late and I couldn't get to a phone, so I decided to wait until the next day for our day off when we'd get to a hotel to call him. When we pulled up to the hotel the next evening, Fletcher came onto the bus while we were sitting around gathering our stuff, waiting to be checked in, and told us that Jason had been found dead of a self-inflicted gunshot wound.

We flew home and attended the memorial service in a daze. Sitting in the bleachers at the local baseball field where we all played as kids, listening to friends and family talk about what a great guy he was, none of it seemed real. We went back out to the

Warped Tour and played to a huge crowd feeling like our hearts had been ripped from our chests. I didn't feel like we should continue playing, as Jason was the soul of our band and the reason I'd joined the group, but we didn't know what else to do, so we just kept going. I didn't have time to stop and process what had happened. At the same time I was dealing with becoming a father for the first time, and all these conflicting pressures and emotions felt like they were closing in on me. There were times when I just picked up my guitar and played until my fingers bled.

Probably the only thing that got me through it was knowing that in a few months time, I was going to be starting a family and that I had to be ready for it, even if inside it felt like everything was spinning out of control. Sometimes I imagined that being a parent would be the easy part, and that dealing with everything else would be what made it overwhelming, but there was no time to focus on that. I had to somehow prepare myself for what I was heading into, even though at the time, I had no idea.

I HATE MY SCHOOL

After going through everything that had happened since Jennifer and I first found out we were having a kid, it felt like we would have to be ready for anything once it started getting closer to our actual due date. I had to admit that I knew very little about childbirth beyond what I'd seen on phony television episodes and what I remembered from my high school sex ed class. Like most things in life, I planned to just fake my way through it and hope for the best. The trouble is, without advance warning, some guys could find out what the word "episiotomy" means and have a total freak-out because some pretty heavy stuff goes down in there. I wanted to get as many facts and as much information as I could going in so I didn't blow it by seeing something unexpected and end up puking all over the delivery room.

These days you can't change the channel without coming across one of those *Live in the ER* cable TV programs that take you up close and personal for an actual birth. When it comes time for the baby to come out and things start stretching out to insane proportions I usually panic and change the channel. When the baby starts crowning, it can pretty much blow your mind completely with how intense, noisy, and messy it is. It isn't pretty, let's just put it that way. Sometimes you hear people talking about how beautiful and wonderful childbirth is, like the baby just arrives on a blanket of gossamer angel wings with harps playing in the background. I guess I can see some beauty in the delivery process in an abstract, theoretical kind of way, but otherwise it can be kind of graphic and horrific for first-time dads. Knowing my propensity to get a little nervous around blood and gore, I decided that I would stand above my wife's shoulder and take in the whole spectacle from above, unlike some guys who get right in on the action and squat down there next to the doctor like they're Mike Piazza waiting on a curveball. For everything else, I could watch as many shows and read as many books as possible, but to get all the necessary information explained in detail, I knew we were going to have to take a birthing class.

Lamaze classes were ridiculous. Mary and I didn't buy into it at all, and we thought the other couples were lame. We knew that the minute it got rough we'd say "Drugs, NOW." and that would be the end of it. We told the people in the first class we planned on naming our daughter Elvis. It was clear from the outset that we were the classroom flu. We spent the rest of the classes proving we deserved the honor.

—Tony Cadena, *The Adolescents*

When we were pregnant with daughter number one we decided to take the Lamaze class the hospital offered that met one night a week for a month. This was our first experience being around other parents and we felt all weird and uncomfortable and out of place because we aren't really the type of people who enjoy sitting around in circles and talking about sexual reproductive organs and telling intimate stories about ourselves with a bunch of complete strangers. I was terrified I would be put on the spot by the teacher and mispronounce some part of the female anatomy and have to explain to the class what a "labia majora" or "mons veneris" was and where it's located.

So luckily, the wife of one of my best friends was also pregnant and they signed up to take the class with us, which was great because we were then able to make sarcastic comments under our breath and giggle like schoolgirls whenever the teachers said things like "scrotum" or "vagina" or showed a slide of any of those things to the class. The class went well until about three-quarters of the way through when the nurse is having the women try different positions for pushing during labor. Most of them are well into their second or third trimester and look like they've just swallowed some type of dodge ball accidentally. The lights in the room are darkened to set a tranquil mood, and everything is very quiet as the men all pretend to murmur encouraging advice and count off for their wives just like it's the real thing. The nurse tells the women to roll over on their sides and try a new position, and starts saying in a quiet, soothing voice, "Just relax, mommies. Relax your body in between contractions and catch your breath. That's it. Good. Relax. Give her encouragement, dads. Tell her what a great job she's doing and how much you love her. That's it. Count for her, dads, help her out. Relax, ladies." Just when the room was so peaceful and quiet you could only hear the barely audible humming of the fluorescent lights above, suddenly I'm startled by a loud blast of flatulence right next to me as my friend's wife accidentally lets rip a powerful fart that splits the still classroom air like a rifle shot in the woods.

There's absolutely no chance everyone in the room, hell, the whole hospital floor, didn't hear it. To her credit, the stoic and professional nurse didn't miss a beat, but she couldn't ignore it, either. "That's totally normal and common to let out a little gas in this position, just everyone continue to relax. Relax and breathe. It's nothing to be concerned about." My friend and I couldn't take it, though. First, he started to giggle, and then the whole class joined in. He said, "Honey, I think you're relaxing a little too much!" We still laugh about it to this day, and I promised my friend's wife I wouldn't put it in the book.

BABY-PROOFING

Once we had separated our anxieties into manageable sections we could stress about one at a time, we had to start getting the house ready for our new arrival. When you are about to have a kid, people will always ask you whether you've baby-proofed your house yet. It seems to me this should mean you have made sure there's no way any crazed babies could break in and steal all your pacifiers and blankies. We spent a lot of time going around the house and covering sharp corners, plugging outlets, and putting safety latches on windows, doors, cabinets, drawers, and cupboards, anything that could slam shut and squash little fingers, even our toilets. We put smoke alarms and carbon monoxide detectors in every room and set the temperature in our water heater so that it couldn't exceed 120 degrees so we didn't accidentally poach the poor kid. Over the years, with three kids, we've become so paranoid that we look at everything in our household as a potential lethal weapon, and my wife goes into our kids' rooms multiple times during the night just to make sure they're still breathing.

The next step was to set up a room for the baby to sleep, play, and crap in, and my job, of course, was putting all the baby furniture together. For some reason most cribs are made in Scandinavian countries that use only their own unique brand of hex head tools, and they usually give you about half the nuts and screws you need to put the thing together. The directions consist of little minimalist line drawing pictures of disembodied hands assembling the hex heads and locking bolts in areas that look nothing like what's in front of you. I sweated through the mind-numbingly difficult task of assembling the damn thing with its thirty million hexagonal nuts and bolts in the living room only to realize that once it was put together it wouldn't fit through the bedroom door. Later on I discovered that it wouldn't fit through the bedroom window, either. Over the years I've found that when assembling any piece of bedroom furniture or complicated toy for my kids, I need to factor in a good three extra hours, accounting for several breaks to go into the garage and drink beer and curse at Swedish furniture makers.

TIME HAS COME TODAY!

I was sound asleep one night because everything was ready to go and I could sleep well knowing we were prepared and so I was dreaming about surfing in turquoise blue water off an island somewhere in the South Pacific and the *Sports Illustrated* swimsuit girls were on the beach waving to me, but *oops!*, one of their tops just accidentally popped off, and the sun was out and warming the little beads of water on my back, and I was ecstatically happy, and then suddenly, one of the swimsuit girls had Jennifer's voice, and she's yelling, "Jim! Jim! Wake up!" Then the light popped on in the bedroom, and I sat bolt upright in the bed and tried to figure out what the hell was going on. My eyes started to focus and I could see my wife standing in the hallway in her nightgown with a pool of clear liquid on the floor between her legs. "What the hell? Did you just piss yourself?"

No, her water just broke in the middle of the night and now without warning my new life as father went from one of theory to one of practice to the real damn thing and my blood pressure instantly went up about 20 percent and hasn't gone back down ever since. I immediately jumped out of bed and started freaking out. Jennifer told me to calm down but I couldn't so I looked around for the bag we'd packed for the hospital, put on my pants, wiped up the mess on the floor, left food out for the cat, and tried to find the keys for the car, and I was doing all these things at the same time so I'm doing them all badly. She was completely calm during all this, which for some reason really pissed me off because I'm not calm at all, and her telling me to be calm is just making me that much more not calm. I finally get everything in the car, called my parents to let them know we're going to the hospital, and then peeled out of the driveway, down the road to the rest of my life.

On Valentine's Day morning at 2 A.M., with my wife sitting on a towel in the passenger seat beside me, I sped through the empty streets of the South Bay and pounded the steering wheel frantically at red lights, finally making it to the doors of Little Company of Mary, the local hospital where I myself had been born decades earlier and where I had been stitched up and treated for various broken limbs, puncture wounds, and food poisonings my whole life. Little Company is a Catholic hospital with sisters and nuns in full head dress roaming the halls, and with statues and paintings of the Virgin Mary solemnly staring down at you everywhere as you pass by. Because our baby was coming out a few weeks premature, when we came rushing in I was tense and worried and agitated and wanted everything as soon as possible, and the lady registering us could probably tell just by looking at me I was going to be a stage-5 stress case the whole time.

When we made our way up to the labor and delivery floor and were meeting the staff for the first time, the head nurse also looked at me a little weird. I suddenly realized how I must have looked at the moment. A few weeks before, I had tried to dye my hair bright red with some vegetable hair dye I got from the local punk store, but I don't think I left it in long enough because in places it had kind of faded into this gross brownish pink color. I hadn't shaved recently and had the remnants of a scruffy beard, and I looked down and realized that I was still wearing the Dead Kennedys shirt I wore to bed that night. I'd always actually admired JFK, but to people not in on the joke, especially those who were around to witness the event on television, wearing a T-shirt making light of an assassinated president pretty much singles you out as a commie-loving flag burner. As she was checking us in and taking our information, the matronly head nurse asked what I did for a living. I cleared my throat and answered that I was the singer of a band called Pennywise. Being my grandmother's age, and from the looks of her, probably not a huge fan of underground skate punk, she, of course, didn't recognize the name and just kind of smiled and said, "Hmm, never heard of it."

Apparently she must have gone out and asked a candy striper about our band and been filled in about how we're this messed-up group of psycho freaks with a guitar player who throws up on people because she came back to the desk with a dismissive smirk on her face and a negative air about her, like all of a sudden she was dealing with monsters from another planet, or draft dodgers, or at least someone whom she knew shouldn't be allowed to be giving birth in the hallowed halls of Our Little Company of Jesus, Mary and Joseph, Super Duper Religious Hospital. She hated us and soon she would be helping deliver our baby.

In Lamaze class we learned that we should ask for the "good room," but I didn't see how it was possible that there could be "good" rooms and "bad" rooms in hospitals. Was one rarely cleaned and infested with plague germs and tumbleweeds, with rusty water dripping from the light fixtures like something out of an old Hitchcock movie, while another was like a spa resort at the Ritz-Carlton? Just by asking for this room, was it like saying the secret password, and they automatically give you a nudge and a wink and begin to treat you like visiting royalty? Because if this wasn't the case, the head nurse who hated me and my Dead Kennedys shirt was definitely not going to be giving us delinquents the good room. No, we'd be giving birth to our spawn of Satan in a remote Siberian outpost wing of the hospital with nothing but a pan of cold water and some salad tongs.

She looked down at her chart and realized regretfully that all of the other rooms were booked, which was punctuated by the fact that a woman was moaning like she was having her toenails removed one by one somewhere nearby, and that by some cruel twist of God's will, we would in fact be getting the "good" room. She looked at the chart again, as if to try to come up with an excuse to put us in an X-ray room or janitor closet somewhere, so she could save the "good" room in case some more pious member of the congregation should stop in and need to deliver their baby. She sighed and realized there was nothing she could do about it, and led the punk rock heathens to their birthing suite.

Truth be told, the good room wasn't that special, the main difference being that it was slightly bigger than some of the other rooms, and was set apart slightly closer to the nurses' desk. I could see how being too close to another room could make yours into a "bad" room if you had a neighbor as vocal as the woman who was still filling the hallways with ear-wrenching shrieks of maternal torment. It was kind of disconcerting to be unpacking our bags and trying to stay calm and positive and setting up our little stereo and scented candles when it sounded like someone was being guillotined slowly with a dull blade in the next room.

We got all settled in, and by this time, Jennifer was having her first contractions and we were just kind of tripping out at what lay ahead of us. When you hear all your friends' harrowing "seventy-two hours in labor" stories, you wonder what the hell could be happening that makes having a baby take so long? Do women really spend two days in the birthing room turning colors and trying to push the kid out for hours on end? Isn't there an easier way to do this? Apparently it can take anywhere from a few hours to several lifetimes, depending on how much God hates you. Jennifer would be sitting there talking to me and then say, "Okay, here comes another one," and then she'd kind of wince and groan and squeeze my hand until it started turning blue for about thirty to forty-five seconds, and then she'd release it with a big sigh. She says it probably feels very similar to that slow, creeping pain like when we get kicked in the balls really hard, except we'd also have to imagine having a ten-pound bowling ball lodged in our spleen, and the groin kicks would have to get increasingly frequent and violent over the next twelve hours.

We found out the reason this process can take so long was that after she was having regular contractions for four or five hours already, and I'd read all the magazines and watched a few dozen infomercials on TV, and was saying things like, "Well, things are moving along nicely, we should be getting close now," the doc would come in and check her dilation and she'd only be at one and a half centimeters, when she needed to get all the way to ten! Then another two or three hours would go by of me wandering the holy halls of Little Company of Mary and poking through cupboards and counting the holes in ceiling tiles and going back and forth to the cafeteria just to be grossed out by the idea of eating food prepared in a place that housed thousands of people with communicable diseases, and then they would come back into our room and check her again and she'd be barely at two! Polar caps have melted faster than this.

I was agitated already and when the nurse gave us the latest reading, I reacted as if I was talking to an old, slow mechanic taking his time giving my car an oil change. "Five hours and we've only advanced a half centimeter? *Are you f-ing kidding me?* She's had sixty-five contractions already and she's nearly broken all the bones in my hand! Isn't there some way we can move this along?" I thought maybe I could slip her a twenty under a bedpan somewhere, and maybe she could give her a laxative or something to pick up the pace a little.

With daughter number one, Jennifer had what's called "pregnancy induced hypertension," which is when you have high blood pressure during the pregnancy or just near delivery. They had planned to induce her two weeks early, but instead she went into labor a week before this. Because her contractions were weak and things were moving so slow, the doctor gave her something to make them stronger and more regular, which, of course, meant more painful. The nurse had her rate her level of discomfort on a scale of one to ten, and then, like a pusher on a downtown street corner, offered her an assortment of different drugs to help out with the pain. They gave her a shot of Nubain, a painkiller that seemed to blunt her sensation somewhat for a while, but a few hours later it wore off, and the second shot didn't work half as well. This is when they brought in the mother of all pain relievers, the epidural, a local anesthetic injected into the spinal column that is supposed to numb the lower half of the body so she doesn't feel the pain as severely. The anesthesiologist comes rolling in like the big pimp sugar daddy on the block, takes out a huge needle, gives her a shot in the back, and all of a sudden she was as happy and carefree as any hippie in the back row of a Grateful Dead concert.

As the labor progressed, though, Jennifer's blood pressure was getting extremely high. I kept watching the monitor and every time it would spike up to a dangerous level, a little warning buzzer would go off and since I'd been running the phrase "died during childbirth" over and over in my head from some western history school book, I would get all panicked and run out to the nurses' desk and yell, "THE BUZZER ALARM THING IS GOING OFF!! I THINK SHE'S DYING!" They would all just look at me weird and say it was okay and not to worry about it and they were watching it. Eventually the doctor gave her magnesium sulfate, which was supposed to help control her blood pressure but also makes you extremely hot and very jumpy. I was nervous already because it was our first child and didn't know what to expect and I was concerned about her blood pressure, thinking her head was going to explode any minute and that I might just have to do a stage dive on the nurses' desk if something didn't start happening soon.

Jennifer was complaining of being boiling hot so I had to keep running back and forth to get ice chips and cold washcloths for her, and this went on for about ten hours of me being worried about her and the baby and watching the monitors and calling the nurse in when the numbers went up too high and the beeping sounds went off. Finally I'd had enough and ran out to the nurses' desk and had a complete meltdown. "LISTEN, WE'VE BEEN HERE FOR FOURTEEN HOURS AND MY WIFE IS BURNING UP AND MY KID COULD BE COOKING LIKE GUMBO IN THERE, SO I NEED ONE OF YOU TO GET UP AND DO SOMETHING ABOUT IT, STAT, BECAUSE THE

BUZZER THING IS FREAKING ME OUT AND I CAN'T DEAL WITH THIS SHIT ANYMORE!" I'm sure half the staff and family members of expectant mothers in the maternity ward were wondering who this strange person was with the Neapolitan hair and the offensive T-shirt and why he was running up and down the halls screaming and freaking out like a mental patient.

After my marathon of anxiety and worry, the doctor came in and checked her, and then like a Delphi Oracle announced that the baby would be delivered at 4 P.M. I looked up at the clock and saw that this was ten minutes away. Was she high? Had she been taking a few shots of Nubain herself? There was no way, with the rate this delivery had been going, that our kid was coming out any time this millennium. I would be here weeks from now having my hand squeezed off with my face glued to the baby monitor.

We soon found out that while the contractions and inactive labor part takes a long-ass time, the actual period of pushing the little punker out is relatively quick in comparison. My mission was to be encouraging and tell her what a great job she was doing and that the baby was almost there. I basically just tried not to be annoying and crack any jokes or point and say, "Oh, my God, how gross!" I sometimes think guys should have a large marble shoved down their pee hole for the pushing part just to experience a little bit of what their wife is going through, but I don't think my idea will get a lot of support from many other prospective fathers out there. I've heard that some women throw up and evacuate their bowels and do a Linda Blair head spin or two during delivery, but my wife just turned a few shades of red, white, and blue in the face, and then let out one loud, guttural rebel yell, worthy of any good punk band, and in a voluminous rush of blood, sweat, and tears, and various other bodily fluids, our baby was born, exactly ten minutes later, just like our doctor had said.

When the baby came out I expected to experience a wide array of emotions: joy, elation, amazement, and maybe even a little nausea and revulsion. I knew some dads weep with joy, while others just do a total face plant on the linoleum and have their infant handed to them in the emergency room while their forehead is being stitched up. For some reason, at first I felt slightly underwhelmed and a little creeped out by the experience. You have to remember newborn babies have been floating in amniotic fluid for the last nine months. You know how when you sit in a Jacuzzi too long your fingers lose all their color and are all shriveled up and gross looking? When they first come out, babies look like this all over and they're covered in all kinds of gunk, blood, and mucus. It's hard to get the big, expected, warm and fuzzy feeling when you are the proud parent of what looks like a Spanish omelet with a face.

Weeks before daughter number one came into the world, when Jennifer was in her third trimester and you could actually see different body parts poking out from her stomach, every night before we fell asleep I started talking to the little critter, figuring me and the new addition should get to know each other a little before the big day. She would lie very still and for some reason this was when the baby became really active, rolling around, jabbing my wife's sides, and punching her bladder like it was a tiny, urine-filled speed bag. I'd start by saying, "Hi, baby! It's Daddy!" to her and she would suddenly become perfectly still, like she stopped whatever she was doing in there to listen to me. Then I would say the ABCs to her a few times. I did this every night without fail until my wife would doze off and wake up later to find me having in-depth conversations with her stomach about Roman architecture and saying, "What I really want to do is direct."

When our first baby girl came out, she was all slimy and crying and freaking out and just totally pissed off to be out of her warm, safe, uterine home and thrust into the cold, harsh light of the real world. Her arms and legs were kicking the air as if to say, "Put me back where I was, this place sucks!" I was standing over my wife's shoulder, and just like I had every night for the last two months, I said to her, "Hi, baby. It's Daddy!" The second she heard my voice, she stopped kicking and moving altogether. She turned her head right toward where I was standing, blinked a few times, and then looked right at me with those perfect baby blue eyes of hers, and that's when I got it, the big rush of adrenaline or endorphins or something indescribable that caused a wave of heat to course through my veins. My breath stopped for a second, and I got the first big, warm, fuzzy feeling of fatherhood looking down at my own real live offspring, a little piece of me and my wife come to life, my own flesh and blood. I thought to myself, "I made that thing. I don't believe it! *That's my kid, dang it!*" I also started thinking about what a screwup I'd been my whole life, how I made my parents' life hell, and how part of me thought I'd never make it out of high school, but now, staring down at this perfect child, I finally got it. *"This is what life's all about. This feeling I'm having looking at my kid."* I'd been looking my whole life for some small bit of meaning in this messed-up world, for something, anything, to believe in, and here it was staring right back at me. All of a sudden, the whole circle of life idea stopped sounding cliché and made perfect sense. Although I didn't do it for security reasons, I wanted to yell out, "HEY, WORLD! THIS IS MY KID! I'M A DAD! I'M NOT A SCREWUP AFTER ALL! CHECK ME OUT!" Then I wanted to go out and buy cigars and do all the stupid stuff dads have done for years to embarrass themselves in hospitals with big goofy grins on their faces.

This is the moment I always try to hold on to whenever I am hit with the crippling anxiety, torturous frustration, and cruel heartache of raising kids. There will be many more like them, where you are in awe of your creation and so proud of them and proud of yourself for having them that you won't care that other people are sick to death of you always talking about the funny thing your kid said and showing them pictures because you just can't stop yourself. But pretty much right after this first moment is when the work begins, as well as the existential worry and hair-pulling stress of parenting that puts you in the spin cycle for the rest of your life.

Two years later, we we're in the same delivery room with daughter number two, and her umbilical cord was wrapped around her neck during delivery. She was stuck in the birth canal and her heart rate was going down every time my wife would have a contraction, and once again I was freaking out and worried but this time the doc and the people on the staff were too. The head nurse finally came up and put her hands on top of Jennifer's stomach and started forcibly pushing the baby out from the outside as hard as she could. Somehow they were able to get her out but the baby's collarbone was broken in the process. I think this might be why daughter number two's such a tough chick. She had to fight and take some pain and punishment to get into this world and now she wants to give some back. Two babies so far and enough delivery room drama for our own sitcom.

Four years after that we were in the female anatomy doctor's office again getting the ultrasound with a four- and six-year-old girl running around among the uterus charts and diagrams, so I thought for sure we'd be having a boy this time. I knew I'd been a bastard to a few girlfriends in high school, but there was no way God would want to punish me so much that he'd make me put three girls through high school and meet hundreds of boyfriends and stay up all night waiting for them to come home and then have to pay for three weddings. That would just be too fucking cruel. The doc, who had three daughters himself, kept asking me if I wanted to know the sex, but I refused. I said, "No way! It has to be a boy this time. I want to wait and be surprised."

It wasn't and I was. Daughter number three came into the world incredibly easy compared to the other two. Jennifer was to be induced this time so instead of being caught off guard in the middle of the night, she got to stroll in on a Saturday morning like she was going in for a teeth cleaning. When we got there they gave us a birthing suite in the new wing they'd just opened on the maternity floor, a spacious luxury hospital condo that Oprah or J.Lo would be proud to deliver in. Our nurse was a hospitable Southern girl who looked like she could have won a Miss America pageant and she treated us like royalty. The doctor was there for the entire day making calls from the hospital so she kept popping in and checking our progress. Before my wife had any pain, they asked if she wanted the epidural, and, of course, she did, and two hours later we had a pain- and stress-free delivery for once. Maybe that's why daughter number three is so mellow.

When it came time to name our kids I thought it might be cool to give our daughters punk rock names, like Peggy Peroxide or Victoria Vomit, but my wife shot me down. I'd always wanted a cool punk name like Ratt Scabies, Darby Crash, or Sid Vicious, but apparently these don't go over as well with kindergarten teachers. I figured that since my wife had carried the kid for nine months and then went through fifteen hours of labor, I should at least let her have the privilege of naming our children. In hindsight, we should have probably given them all conservative Republican names like Nancy or Barbara just to anticipate the inevitable parental backlash.

THE PUNK ROCK NAME GENERATOR

You've heard of the name-generating systems in which you combine two things to come up with a specific name—for example, your porn star name is your childhood pet's name and the street you grew up on (Genève Cornell, Bootsey Broadway, etc.). Well, here is how you find the perfect baby punk rock name: your middle name plus an infectious disease that you or someone in your family has contracted, preferably some kind of disgusting skin ailment, for example—

Vinnie Vitiligo

Eddie Eczema

J. T. Boil

Alexis Angioma

Donnie Dermatitis

Iggy Impetigo

Sally Psoriasis

Rosey Rosacea

Danny Dandruff

Richard "Dick" Diphtheria

Harry Hepatitis

Freddy Influenza

Bonnie Botulism

Colin Cholera

Rita Gonorrhea

Stephen Ring Worm

Julio Polio

Milo Monkey Pox

Phyllis Syphilis

Alexander Acne

Our first experience in the delivery room, I was so stressed and out of my head I was probably a total pain to deal with, so with daughters two and three I knew better. I greeted everyone nicely, asked questions, took names, and put people on my Christmas card list. I joked with the janitor and told the old lady checking us in that her nurse's smock really brought out the blue in her eyes. Everyone loved me. The reason I learned I needed to kiss some ass at the hospital is because like any other service provider it's up to the staff to decide just what type of service they're going to provide. If you're nice and cordial and complimentary, you could get the "good" room, but if you come in trying to be hard and punk and antisocial, you and your wife will be sent to a desolate corner of the hospital with five hundred other wailing mothers, an army cot for a bed, and you'll have a witch doctor from Barbados delivering your baby.

After we had our first kid my whole life took on a whole new brilliance and sense of urgency. I had this nagging suspicion that I didn't have time to screw around anymore. The father protector/provider instinct started welling up inside me, and suddenly life was about something more besides drinking beer, bashing into people in the slam pit, and screaming at the top of my lungs at punk gigs. I knew I had to begin to sacrifice my own immediate needs to those of my kids and that there was a lot of work to be done. To everyone else, I probably appeared my normal, carefree self, but inside I was becoming a completely different person. When I was happy, I was ecstatically f@#king happy. When I was pissed off, I could tear the bark off trees with my bare hands and eat it. When I was sad, I could cry ancient floods of salty, wet tears. This is what having kids did to me.

When I wrote songs about wanting to change the world, I meant it more than ever, because now there was a lot more than my own miserable future at stake, and that something needed its diaper changed regularly and food put on the table every day. I was now a certified, not to be trifled with, punk rock dad.

3

HEY, HO! LET'S GO!

Once we'd delivered our first bundle of joy and our friends and parents had dropped off their flowers and obnoxious metallic balloons and the doctor made sure the baby had "voided," they strapped the little one into our car seat and set us off on the ride of our life. One day I didn't have a care in the world, my only concern being the next time the Circle Jerks or T.S.O.L. were playing and rearranging my album collection into pre- and post-Minor Threat years, the next I woke up to a screaming infant who had to have its needs catered to at every moment. There were diapers to change, feeding issues to decide, and I soon found out that I wouldn't be sleeping very much at all for several weeks. This was not a test. This was the real thing, and our crash course in parenting 101 had officially begun.

Right after we walked through the door with our new baby, it felt like a completely different place. From then on, our senses were always at a heightened state of alert. "What is the baby doing? Is it crying? Is it hungry? Is it sleeping? Does it have a poopy diaper? Is it surfing the Internet for porn? What the hell is going on?" Guys usually need a little more time to adjust to a new environment but I didn't have that luxury. The first few days out of the hospital were all about me and the baby because the wife felt like an eighteen-wheeler just rolled over her crotch and she needed to take a load off for a while. She seemed great and cheerful at the hospital, but once she got home and realized what she'd been through, she crawled into bed and didn't feel like getting out for a couple of days. It was on-the-job training at its best, and my initial task was playing baby interpreter to try and figure out what the baby needed and when she needed it.

THIRSTY AND MISERABLE

The first few days with a newborn are kind of like what I imagine it must've been like to be the tour manager for the Sex Pistols: You just waited around to see what the next crisis would be. When we came home from the hospital, Jennifer's milk hadn't come in yet, and the baby would suck away and not get much of anything. She tried to assure me that this was okay and that the small bit of colostrum the baby would get whenever she would nurse was enough to tide her over until her milk came in, but I wasn't buying it. It seemed to me that the little bean couldn't possibly be getting enough food to survive and would soon shrivel up and starve like one of those Hollywood starlets that live off Diet Coke and gum. I was also concerned because she hadn't taken a bowel movement yet and I knew that if she didn't soon, we'd have to take her back to the hospital because she'd begin to develop jaundice, which is when they get so backed up they actually start turning colors like a little Oompa Loompa. I was worried that with nothing going in and nothing coming out, we'd somehow brought home a defective baby that couldn't eat or evacuate its bowels on its own. Every time she made a noise, I'd grab her out of her bassinet, rush her to Jennifer, and tell her we had a noneating, nonpooping baby and that she had to do something.

Thankfully, after a while, my wife's boobs suddenly filled up with milk and got rock hard, and the baby started sucking away. Once this first crisis was averted and she had eaten her fill, we went back to worrying that she hadn't evacuated her bowels yet and that soon we'd be back in the hospital with our little yellow baby roasting under heat lamps for two days. We were hovering over her, concerned while she was laying on her back on the changing table, when she made a strange face and then exploded a giant shat that sprayed all over our faces and the walls around us. With baby poo dripping off her nose, Jennifer said, "Oh, thank God."

After all the stress and pressure of bringing home a newborn, we were both ready for a nice, long, well-needed rest. We figured she would just pass out on her own eventually and sleep for hours, but we had a rude awakening when that first night, as we both laid down in bed, daughter number one stayed awake from midnight until six in the morning. The next night she did the same thing, and then again the next night after that, and the night after that. We were slowly devastated to find over the next few weeks that she didn't want to sleep at night for more than a couple of hours at a time, ever. Just when we were dying for a few continuous hours of shut-eye ourselves, she wanted to stay up all night and party.

Like clockwork, we'd hear her starting to make noises in her bassinet. Then she'd start getting cranky because no one was coming to get her, and then she'd just bust out and start bawling hysterically. The wife and I would both lay perfectly still and pretend to be asleep, hoping to God the other would get up and entertain her, until finally one of us would give up, rip off the sheets, and pick her up, the whole time muttering a long stream of profanities. After a few weeks of this, we started to wonder if we'd given birth to some kind of crazed baby insomniac who would never sleep and instead just roam the hallways at night like a baby vampire.

We slowly came to find out that, as parents of an infant, most of the time would be spent monitoring the eating, sleeping, and pooping habits of our newborn. It seemed like they were always in the process of doing one or the other and when they weren't we were always concerned why. During this time you find out a lot about yourself, and I found that I'm extremely impatient. Instead of being a help to Jennifer, I just stressed her out by being the bodily functions-obsessed baby monitor.

"Honey, it's three o'clock and she hasn't taken a crap yet."

"I'm sure she's fine."

"When did you feed her last?"

"A couple of hours ago."

"Did she eat enough?"

"As much as she wanted."

"Shouldn't you feed her again to help move things along?'"

"Not if she's not hungry."

"Does she need a nap then?"

"Not if she's not sleepy."

"Well, she's just lying there making gurgling sounds and staring at me and not doing anything."

"That's what most babies do."

"Couldn't we just give her a cup of coffee or something? That always works for me."

"Don't you need to write a song or go on tour or something?"

BREASTFEEDING

Let's face it, if there are two things most guys know for sure about ourselves, it's that we're lazy and we like boobs. If you can somehow talk your partner into breastfeeding, you'll have a lot less to do the first year and her boobs will be several sizes bigger. I knew that with bottle feeding there would be a lot of washing and cleaning and sterilizing of bottles, nipples, and rings and boiling of water and any time I helped out, my wife would be circling around me the whole time telling me what I was doing wrong. I'd read somewhere that there's more and more evidence that breast milk may help fight infections by boosting the immune system, and that it can lower the risk of certain ailments for both mom and the baby, and so I tried to stress all these important factors for my wife to consider, but the truth was I really wanted to save myself some work and see what her boobs looked like several sizes bigger. This is a delicate situation because not all women are comfortable with or even capable of breastfeeding, so I tried to do everything I could to help out and be supportive, short of getting down there and sucking away myself, although I've heard some dads are into that. It's a little too Oedipal for me, personally.

During her pregnancy, Jennifer had perused all the best maternity stores and websites to make sure she had the most up-to-date gadgetry needed for modern-day child care. She ordered an expensive machine off the Internet called a breast pump, which women use to suck the milk out of their breasts to freeze and save for later when needed. Seeing your girl using this contraption will either send you into therapy or make you laugh your ass off. It's a funny-looking, noisy black box that sounds like it has a Volkswagen motor in it that sucks the milk out of her boobs with two little suction cups and makes her look exactly like a human cow at a dairy farm. No girl on the face of the earth wants to be told she looks like a cow even when she is sitting on the edge of the bed having milk extracted from her teats. This machine, funny and noisy as it was, became very useful for freezing some bottles for me to use later, when she'd gone out with the girls because I'd told her she looked like a cow.

One of the things I loved about breastfeeding besides me not having to do anything was that when the baby was hungry, no matter where we were, we were always prepared. Mom just whipped one out, covered up, and she was a walking buffet. We didn't have to worry about having a bottle washed and ready or the right amount of formula and sterile water; we could do it anywhere, in restaurants, at the grocery store, in the park, who cares? That being said, I didn't want my wife to be one of these nature woman-granola moms who sit around topless at the playground with a set of four-year-old twins latched onto each boob, expecting everyone to be cool with it, but when it was appropriate, why not? The problem was figuring out when it was appropriate.

We were out at a local Italian restaurant once when the baby started crying, and Jennifer said she was probably getting hungry.

"Well, go ahead and feed her," I said. "No one will care."

"I should just go out to the car. There's an older couple over there staring at us and they might not approve."

Sitting across from us at a table were a man and a woman who looked liked they'd just left a Republican fund-raiser. He was in a dark blue pin-striped suit and she was in a dinner dress and pearls, and they were both silently eating their Caesar salads and sharing a bottle of wine.

"Oh, come on. Just cover up with the tablecloth a little bit, they won't be able to see."

She relented and when the baby started nursing, I saw the lady across from us make a disgusted face and whisper something to her husband. I couldn't hear her, but I imagined she was telling him to take a look at the dirty hippies breastfeeding their kid in a public restaurant. As a youth I was never afraid to fly the punk rock flag by occasionally wearing the standard uniform of plaid bondage pants, bleached spiked hair, and three-inch creepers, so I'd grown accustomed to having conservative types look down and scoff at me as a vile street hoodlum, even though I knew this was the furthest thing from the truth. Coming from a middle-class family in an affluent beach suburb and always getting everything I wanted for birthdays and Christmas, I was hardly your typical juvenile delinquent street punk, but I liked the feeling of being seen by the establishment as an outsider, as Derby Crash sang: a "puzzled panther waiting to be caged." Now it was my turn to be disgusted.

I sneered to Jennifer with my best Billy Idol scowl. "Can you believe these Reaganomic, Bible thumpin' snobs looking down their noses at us just because you're breastfeeding? Is it so wrong for a couple to want to feed their baby in a restaurant when she's hungry, while they sit over there stuffing their faces after a third trip to the salad bar?"

"Oh, big deal, don't make a scene."

"No, I mean it. What do we have to be ashamed of? This is a free country, and until there's a law passed by one of their heavily lobbied congressmen cronies saying women can't do what nature intended and breastfeed their child in public restaurants, we should be able to do it right out in the open. I say you should whip your shirt off right now and go tits to the wind just to show these puritans that we still believe in the Constitution and women's rights. What are they so afraid of, that they might get flashed a nipple and lose their religion? These people make me sick."

My wife knows that sometimes when I get on my high horse she has to just let me ride and take a few laps before I calm down. Just when I was ready to leap up on the table and whip down my own pants in the name of free speech and the first amendment, I noticed the gentleman across the way calling the waiter over and telling him that their wine had gone bad and they didn't want it. Later on when they were finished, they walked by our table and said what a cute baby we had. I finished my meal knowing our baby was well fed and that the Constitution was safe.

DOOKIE

After feeding the baby, the next thing we always had to be aware of was when the kid had taken a little baby dump in its diaper. With our first encounter with a full diaper, we were extremely proud and wanted to call all our friends and bring the neighbors over to show them what our little gastronomic genius had done in her diaper, but we tried to refrain from doing this. Of all the cute baby stories, the ones people hate hearing the most are the ones about the cute little crap your kid took. It's only cute to you, trust me. Later on, they weren't so cute anymore and I had to master the art of not breathing for several minutes at a time to stifle my gag reflex, and my relationship with my wife became one where I was constantly coercing, negotiating, and ro-sham-bo-ing her into taking my turn changing the next diaper. It consumed our lives.

My problem was that, just like my complete inability to fold a T-shirt or pair of pants, at first I had real difficulties putting a diaper on the baby. My hands, thumbs, and fingers just didn't seem to be able to work together to perform the task. My wife thought I was feigning incompetence just to get out of doing it, but I think I was just physically incapable of it. I would have just went through the torture of unbuckling and taking off the blue jean overalls, and unsnapped the five hundred snaps on the onesie, and recovered from the ungodly smell, and then cleaned and wiped up the skid marks from all the nooks and crannies and baby folds, and swabbed everything down, and then it's time to put on a new diaper. But the baby is wriggling around too much and they always pull their legs up and try to stick their feet in their mouth when they're on their back so you have to hold their legs down with one hand and try to strap the diaper on with the other, and the diaper has to be positioned just right but it never is because the baby's butt is squirming all over the place. Then, when you pull one side over and Velcro it on and try to do the other, the first side pops open, then the legs go back up, and then it's done finally, except both legs are out one hole and I had to use duct tape to get it to stay closed. Then I resnap the five hundred snaps on the onesie again and rebuckle the blue jean overalls and as soon as I'm done, I hear a really wet fart down there and realize I just have to do it all over again.

Even though I was horrible at diaper changing at first, I knew that in the age of shared duties and responsible parenting I'd be expected to take turns and do my fair share of wet cleanups. My wife started to notice that I would always be conspicuously absent, rushing out to the garage like I'd just been hit with inspiration, whenever the stench of a full diaper suddenly wafted into the room. We worked out a trade-off where if I did some task she hates doing, like cleaning the toilets, or if I agreed to go in her place to some boring school function, she'd work toxic cleanup for the next five changes. This way, I'm doing my part but also getting out of the hostile environment of poo management in the process. She's probably only willing to barter this way because I take so long changing the diaper, and complain about it so much while I'm doing it, and make a huge mess that she'd rather do it herself. After a while, though, I became so good at it I could do it with my eyes closed, and after seeing the horror that can come out of a child's body, sometimes I wanted to.

We soon found out that the most important tool in our arsenal of baby care supplies was a box of baby wipes. At one point I wanted to go out and buy an entire truck load because over the next several years, our box of wipes became our most valued and trusted best friend. We'd keep a box in every room of the house, the bedrooms, bathrooms, garage, tool shed, everywhere. We'd keep a few boxes in each of our cars and stash one or two at our parents' and friends' houses in the planter or hedges, without them knowing, for emergencies. We'd even bury a few boxes in the sand when we went to the beach. Once, during a particularly messy potty training episode, I made myself a little baby wipes holster so I could whip one out at a moment's notice.

Once when we were all out at a California Pizza Kitchen at the local mall, just as we were seated, the baby filled her diaper, which was readily apparent because the smell drifted throughout the entire dining area like a cloud of mustard gas in World War I, and one by one the families at the tables surrounding us made disgusted faces and covered their noses and gave us dirty looks, as if their children had never filled their diapers in a crowded restaurant before. I scooped up the offending child and took her out to the minivan, which I'd just given its monthly turbo cleaning: having taken out all the stray bottles, sippy cups, Barbie dolls, and stuffed animals, vacuumed up all the cracker crumbs, bagel bites, and granola bars that had been smashed into the carpet, and swabbed down all the imitation leather seats. I laid the baby down on the passenger seat, undid the Velcro diaper tabs, and was confronted by an incredibly full volcanic diaper that spilled out everywhere, down the sides, up the back, and onto my newly cleaned imitation leather seats.

Immediately I looked around for a box of baby wipes but then remembered, *Turbo Cleaning Day!* In an effort to make the minivan spotlessly clean, I had taken out all the boxes of baby wipes and forgotten to replace them. Along with most of her body, all the baby's clothing was covered in baby poo, so I stripped her down completely and then suddenly realized I had nothing new to clothe her in. I picked her up and for a while just stood there at a loss for what to do next. I had nothing to wipe her up with, and I couldn't just stroll back into the restaurant with a naked baby covered in shit from the shoulders down and pretend everything was normal. If you had been driving through the Manhattan Village Mall on this fateful autumn night, you might have seen me at the back of a minivan having a total emotional breakdown, holding a half-naked child who looked like it had sat ass-first in a pot of chili con carne.

It seemed that my children would save their bowel movements of Biblical proportion for these inopportune moments of need. It couldn't be one of the times when a tidy little dry turd the size of a hamster pellet comes out. No, the time I misplace my last box of wipes is when I'm treated with the ones that look like a mud slide on P.C.H. in Malibu. So now, you panic. Most parenting books will tell you to be patient and try to stay calm, but I think this is a situation where it's okay to just lose it completely and curl up in a ball and cry because there's no easy way out of it. After this episode I bought enough baby wipes to cover a small foreign country and saved myself a world of pain.

SLEEP

After eating and pooping, the other thing our first baby did was sleep, but not as often as we hoped. Weren't babies just supposed to go down for the night peacefully at seven or eight o'clock, and only wake up for a quick fifteen-minute feeding or two and then go back to sleep? If so, why was my kid always still wide awake at 2:30 A.M., and why hadn't either of us had our eyes closed for more than a few minutes since she was born? Every day it seemed to get harder and harder to get her to finally go to sleep, and we'd have to do all kinds of crazy things to try and get her to nod off, from driving her around the block in the car for hours, pathetically waving to the neighbors each time we passed them watering their lawn, to wearing tracks in the carpet walking circles around the house, bouncing her up and down and nearly giving myself a hernia in the process. She'd eventually fall asleep, but as soon as I stopped bouncing or walking, she'd let out a huge scream and wake up again.

With all this late-night and early-morning activity, I tried to remember how when I was younger and I could stay out all night and party no problem, the hours seemed to just fly by and before I knew it, the sun was coming up. When you are sitting on the couch staring at the TV station color bars and listening to nothing but the absolute quiet, dead of night, and you're drooling and nodding off, but your kid is still jumping up and down in its bouncer, the hours tend to creep by a little more slowly. I'd be walking around downtown after the fifth consecutive all-nighter with the insomniac, and people would have no trouble coming up to me and saying, "Dude, you look like shit!" and I did look like shit. My hair was matted on my head, I had permanent sheet marks on my face and my eyes were always puffy and bloodshot with huge carry-on luggage bags underneath them. I think I personally started the whole bed head hairstyle just by walking around in public after only getting an hour of sleep the night before.

Eventually we got her to start going to sleep at a semireasonable hour and taking short naps in the day, but she was always waking up and fighting going down, and keeping us up all hours. To this day, she's the last to go to bed, rarely sleeps through the night, and every morning I'm woken up by her standing beside my bed, pulling my eyelids open, saying, "Daddy, wake up!" Number two was only slightly better, but she at least would sleep through the night once we got her down. With number three, we were finally blessed with a child who sleeps like a rock, goes to bed early, wakes up late, and will instantly nod off for long naps throughout the day. The problem is we rarely get to enjoy it since we're always having to keep her up late, wake her up early, and interrupt her naps for the nonstop shuttling of the older kids to sports and school-related activities. Sometimes I go on tour now just to catch up on my sleep. Lucky for us, when our kids don't get enough sleep and become overtired, angry, and cranky, nature has provided them with a time-proven method of letting us know about it.

CRYING

If God is really mad at you for something you did in high school, you might get a baby with 'colic,' which is apparently when your baby spends most of its waking hours screaming at the top of its lungs. The scream of the colicky child isn't like an "I want something to eat" whining cry, or the "There's something wet and gross between my legs" annoyed moan; it sounds as if they are being dunked in boiling water or they've just seen a headless body behind you. Their little lips tremble and their whole body shakes and the more you try to get them to stop once they've worked up a ball of steam, the more pissed off they get. This can be a parent's worst nightmare.

I wouldn't go so far as to say daughter number one had colic, but she could sure let it rip when she wanted to. Sometimes during the day I'd have to walk around with headphones on, listening to G.B.H. just to try and drown it out. No luck. The crying went on and on, sometimes through the night. There were times when we just had to let her cry it out. I'd go in the garage and start playing my guitar, testing just how loud my Marshall stack could go without getting the cops called. When I would pause for a moment or segue into a dramatic breakdown, in the background through the walls I could still hear her wailing away like mad. I think this is why our fourth album has so few breaks in the action. If I stopped playing, I'd hear the crying again.

The incessant nature of it began eating away at my sanity. There were some days when she had been crying so much that I just wanted to start crying right along with her. I tried to consider it a test of just how much pain I could tolerate, like getting a tattoo across your entire back or several eyebrow and nose piercings. I meditated and read Buddhist verses and searched for ways to manage my stress that didn't include a fifth of Jack Daniels or an eight-foot bamboo bong.

After a few weeks I started to become an expert at knowing which cry was for when the baby was hungry, which was for when she was tired, and which was for when she was just sick of me making baboon faces at her all day. I heard so much crying I became a connoisseur. At a certain point, my ears eventually started to become somewhat numb to the sonic frequency of a crying baby. I could hear it, but it didn't annoy me as much after I'd listened to it night and day for several months. We would go on tour, I'd be sitting in a restaurant or on a plane with a baby screaming bloody murder right next to me, and I wouldn't be bothered in the slightest. People around me are freaking out and I can't hear a thing, all because I have three kids.

Babies cry. That's what they do. It's usually their way of saying something isn't right, but sometimes it can be for no reason at all except sheer boredom, and letting out a big cry at the cold hopelessness of the world feels good when you've been in a nice warm womb for the last nine months having all your needs attended to. Nine times out of ten, the baby just wants to be picked up and held. Imagine being the size of a loaf of bread and feeling totally helpless; you'd cry occasionally too. We older folk are the ones who repress the biological need to let out a good long wail every once in a while, which is why most of us turn to therapy or alcohol or become lead singers in punk bands so we can scream our lungs raw every night. We all need to bitch and complain about the world and our predicaments in it—babies just have a better way of vocalizing it.

IT'S JUST ME & YOU, KID!

After going through that first emotionally and physically wrenching childbirth, and the first few months of dealing with dirty diapers, painful breastfeeding, and baby insomnia, the wife needed a night out with people who weren't the baby or me. This was my first opportunity to show I was responsible enough to be left alone with our child and have us both somehow survive the experience. As she was leaving, my wife ran down a detailed list of everything I needed to do and remember, including defrosting a bottle of breast milk that she'd pumped using the motorized milk extractor by putting the frozen bottle in a coffee mug and running hot water from the tap over it, then checking it religiously to make sure it was exactly room temperature before I fed it to her. If I wanted, I could give her a bath in the infant tub, but not with too much water because if I turn my back on her for a second when she's in it she could drown. I was to constantly watch her and make sure she wasn't choking on something and that she was still breathing. When she was ready to sleep I had to lay her down on her back because otherwise she could die of SIDS and I shouldn't put her on my chest while I watch TV on the couch because I might fall asleep and smother her. She'd written down the name, address, and phone number of the place they were going and everyone she'd be with and lots of other carefully worded warnings, and I whisked her out the door telling her to have a good time and that I had everything handled.

I'd been helping out and doing my share of baby duties and knew I had everything under control so this was just going to be a nice, relaxing night with me and my daughter hanging out together, having a good time watching the tube and kicking it on the couch. While she was sitting in her little vibrating bouncy unit, gurgling and trying to bite her toes, I made myself a TV dinner and we settled in for a nice uneventful evening, when right as I took my first bite she started to fuss a little bit so I went over and showed her a little stuffed teddy bear and she liked that for a minute but then she got sick of it and started fussing again and so I started making faces at her and she looked at me strangely for a while but that didn't help much and she started crying again and so I decided to pick her up and take her out of her bouncer but when I picked her up her little leg was caught on the belt that held her in and I tried to hold her and unbuckle it but I couldn't do both at the same time and she kind of slipped a little and so I picked her back up but the whole chair came with her and was hanging from her leg and she knew something wasn't right with this picture and even though she's only a couple of months old she gives me a look like, *"You don't know what the fuck you're doing do you?"*, then takes a few deep breaths and starts crying in earnest.

So I unhook her from the bouncy seat and start to dance her around a little and say, "You want to hear some music?'" and I saunter over to the stereo and turn on the CD player, but apparently I had it up pretty loud last time because the sound of a radio commercial comes blasting out of the speakers and scares the living shit out of both of us, and now she's looking at me even more nervously and crying harder. I quickly turn it down and switch to the CD player and it starts playing "Sheena Is a Punk Rocker" by the Ramones, and she instantly starts to calm down. She must recognize the music because I'm always playing this album when I'm doing the dishes or fixing something around the house. I start to dance her around a little and we're listening to Johnny and Joey and Dee Dee blasting away and we're bouncing off the furniture having our own little father-daughter slam pit.

As we begin slamming around the living room together, she starts cracking up and laughing her ass off. I then start imitating all the different slam dance styles I've witnessed over the years. I do the guy who bobs his head back and forth like he's doing the funky chicken, and she loves that one. Then there's the flour grinder who flails his arms all over the place, trying to take out as many people as he can, the East Coast picking up change move, and the casual guy who cruises around the pit like he's on a Sunday stroll, daring anyone to bump into him. (If there's one thing our generation of bands has contributed to the punk scene, it's that we brought slam dancing to a global scale. When mosh pits were just about a few punks bashing into each other at CBGB's, now there are twenty thousand people slamming in a mosh pit as big as most parking lots. It's pointless, ridiculous, and most would say stupid, but also a lot of fun.) With each different dance she's laughing harder and harder and that giggle of hers is like music to my ears, and in my tiny living room we're having our own little daddy-daughter punk rock show.

After going through most of the Ramones album and into the Dickies and Toy Dolls, two of her other favorites, we fall down on the couch exhausted. I figure she must be hungry and it's time for her to eat so I bring her into the kitchen, get out the frozen bottle of breast milk from the freezer, and put it into a coffee mug and start running hot water over it, but it's hard to do with one hand so I put her back in her bouncer and she doesn't want me to put her down and starts to cry but I need to get her milk ready so she's just going to have to yell for a while. I quick boil some water and put the bottle in there so it starts defrosting a lot faster and it looks like it's working so I squirt some on the inside of my wrist like my wife does and it's boiling fucking hot like hot coffee and now I have to cool it off under the cool water and check it again but I can't tell if it's cooled down enough yet because who says the inside of your wrist is such an accurate temperature gauge and so I'm squirting it on my arm and my thigh and my stomach and even take a few shots in my mouth and *man* that stuff tastes weird like sweet body milk mixed with sweat but it seems like it's close to room temperature and so I give it to her and when she finally calms down enough she starts sucking it right down and we can both relax for a minute.

After she's done, I put her on my shoulder and she lets out a giant burp that sounds like a barge coming into the harbor, and then gives me a little smile afterward. It must be the same feeling of relief I get letting out a belch like a long dormant volcano after eating a bratwurst and drinking a pint of Guinness. I decide to give her a bath in the tub and I'm amazed at how slippery a little soapy infant can be, because there are times when I can't even seem to get a good grip on her. At one point I turn my back and look for the baby soap and then turn back around and she's somehow managed to twist around and flip over in the tub. I grab her quick and realized I'd nearly drown my kid in about two inches of water. She gives me the "you're a complete moron" look again but somehow she recovers without freaking out and she's blowing little fart bubbles in the water every once in a while and I'm putting suds in her hair and giving her a little Mohawk and we're both having a good time. I just splash her off a little more and get her out because I'm afraid she's going to slip out of there like a cherry pit and go sliding across the floor. I dry her off and now it's time for diapers and a sleeper and hopefully she can fall asleep.

I go into the baby's room and search through the drawers, through all the thousands of different kinds of baby clothes, the fuzzy sleepers with teddy bears and furry bunnies on the front, and tiny baby T-shirts with Misfits skulls and "Little Punk" logos, and finally find the proper onesie with its eighteen hundred snaps and attempt to put it on her. This is never an easy task with all her limbs flailing around everywhere, and more than once I get her two arms out the neck hole so it looks like she's wearing a little baby tube top and get the perturbed look from her again, but eventually I coax her into it, even though something about the way it was fitting her still looks a little strange. Onesies are cool and comfortable and babies spend most of their early lives cruising around in them and I had to admit that I secretly coveted the onesie and wondered if they came in men's size 36.

Now that she's fed, cleaned, and ready for bed and beginning to look tired, I start bouncing her up and down, trying to get her to fall asleep until finally I give up and lay down on the couch with her. Luckily she's not fussing much and is just kind of laying there, looking up at me, and I wonder how she can be this close to me and not be repulsed by my large pores and garlic breath but for some reason she still likes me and is gazing up at me with those perfect eyes of hers again until she starts blinking and begins drifting off to sleep. As she lays there I'm looking down at her and realizing this is what they mean when they talk about unconditional love, and that even though I'm not very good at it, I'm her dad and she's my kid, and we're stuck with each other and will be forever and nothing can ever change that no matter what happens. It's one of those perfect moments where nothing else matters except me and my kid laying there together and Alex Trebek is talking about "potent potables" in the background and the wind is blowing softly outside and everything's peaceful and quiet, but then the next thing I know, my wife is shaking me, yelling, "Jim, Jim! Wake up, you moron, you fell asleep again!" I jump up thinking I squashed the baby or someone had kidnapped her, but thank God my wife was holding her and she seemed fine, if just a little frazzled and confused again.

So I rub my eyes and look around and say, "What d'ya mean? Everything's fine, we had a great time. Look how happy she is. Why'd you wake her up?"

Then my wife says, "Do you realize you put her onesie on upside down?"

"What?"

"You didn't notice that instead of it looking like she's wearing a normal sleeper, it looks like she has a turtleneck on top, and cowboy chaps on the bottom?"

It seems that every time I watch the kids I do a great job and we have a great time together, but there's always that one little thing my wife notices when she gets home, the water left on in the bath tub or the child playing with the curtain cord or a bucket of rusty nails, and it's these little oversights that somehow make me look totally incompetent.

Eating, sleeping, diapers, and crying were some of the bigger challenges in this period of our child's development. I tried to go through them with a cool head and make it a test to see just how mellow and controlled I could be when things got really stressed. When the baby shit really hit the fan though, I'd calmly tell the wife that I needed a little "me" time, and I'd get the paper and find out where there was a punk show going down that night, and when I'd get there I'd go into the slam pit and wreak bloody havoc. I'd own that pit until no one dared enter for fear of colliding with the stressed out dad who'd changed one too many diapers on a screaming baby. I did this one night and got my nose broken and it felt really good. I'd drive home feeling refreshed, rejuvenated, and ready for the challenges that lie ahead.

THE GLAMOUROUS LIFE OF A WARPED TOUR VETERAN

"My daughter Violet slept with my wife and me until she was two years old, mainly because it made breastfeeding easier. She pretty much goes for it all day until she passes out. It's chaos. Touring is not all that different. You don't sleep, you get thrown up on, people throw bottles at your face, sometimes you shit or piss in your pants, and you're drunk every night. It's fun."

—**Joey Cape**, *Lagwagon*

After the first few months, we had settled into a routine with daughter number one and it was time for me to be back out on the road to play the Vans Warped Tour and deal with my own version of morning sickness. The Warped Tour covers about fifty cities in about fifty-five days, which means about three days off in two months and traveling from L.A. to Vancouver to Boise to Detroit, San Antonio, Virginia Beach, Rykers Island, and every stifling hot city in between. There are about a hundred bands of old school and new school punk, emo, screamo, hardcore, thrash, metal, rap, DJs, and shit that can't be qualified into any category, all on half a dozen stages along with hundreds of merch booths, food stands, skate ramps, climbing walls, and moto jumps, and if you're a skate punk kid with tattoos and body piercings it's a wet dream.

When we were out surviving the Warped Tour, every other day or so I'd call my wife and ask her how the baby was doing and she'd tell me that she was fine but that they had a doctor checkup that day and when they stripped the baby down and put her on the scale to weigh her, she produced a loud stream of flatulence and filled her diaper right in front of the doctor and to a person somewhat socially shy like my wife this was catastrophically embarrassing, and when she's catastrophically embarrassed, she tends to start giggling uncontrollably and can't stop and begins turning red, which is what happened and the doctor probably thought she was mental. Otherwise she was okay and so she asks me how the tour is going.

A typical day on the Warped Tour goes something like this. You wake up in your bunk around noon and you're sweating like a pig because the air-conditioning went off on your side of the bus and your face has five thousand lines engraved in it because you had to use someone's pants for a pillow last night because someone stole yours. You immediately stumble out of your bunk because the combined smell of the feet, farts, and jock fungus of twelve guys who have been eating nothing but barbecue for the last five weeks has been mixing in the poorly ventilated sleeping area, and now the rancid air you've been inhaling all night finally registers with your olfactory senses and you throw up in your mouth a little at the stench of it. You look out the window and have no idea where you are because all you see are other buses sandwiched in as close as possible on all sides. You surmise that you must be in a stadium parking lot somewhere in Cleveland, but it might as well be Detroit, or Chicago, or Milwaukee, because all these places are starting to look the same, but one thing's for sure, you know that you need to find some coffee and a bathroom, but not necessarily in that particular order.

You can hear that there are no less than five bands playing at the same time on several stages surrounding you, because the throbbing of the bass and kick drum has just reminded you that you drank way too much last night, because what the hell else is there to do but drink way too much when you're on a traveling music festival with fifty other bands and crew? So every night someone has a barbecue and you start with a few beers in between chicken wings and cheeseburgers and then there's

Bloody Marys on somebody's bus and maybe someone's opened a bottle of red wine, or worse, Jameson's, and the next thing you know you're shit faced, and why not, because how in the world could you be sober in an extreme action sports and music, testosterone-fueled traveling circus festival and retain any shred of sanity?

So here it is the next day and you're hung over again and you step off the bus into daylight and it's well over a hundred degrees outside because why wouldn't it be? You're in a stadium parking lot, in the middle of some U.S. city downtown, in the middle of the day, in the middle of summer, so of course it's hot, hotter than any human should be forced to endure for more than ten or twenty seconds before darting back into an air-conditioned room, but all you can think about is that at some point during the day, instead of sitting in an air-conditioned room like most people should be doing on a 100-degree day, you are going to get up on a stage in front of about fifteen thousand equally hot and sweaty young people and spaz out as much as you possibly can for forty minutes until you start seeing double and begin to hallucinate.

Right now, however, you need to find a bathroom and since you can't go number two on the bus you have to find a Port-a-Potty, but there is none in sight so you go around and meet other band members and crew, who, like you, look and smell horrible, and they are also walking funny and looking around with one eye open, squinting against the harsh noonday sun, and then a straight edge tour manager finally points you in the right direction and you find the one open Port-a-Potty and you are so happy and you go in the door and it plasticly slams behind you. It's pitch-black dark, and it's at least twenty degrees hotter in there than it is outside, and then that's when it hits you, the smell. The smell is there. Your eyes haven't adjusted but the smell is already making you see colors. It has shape. It is a monster. It hits you in the solar plexus and takes your breath away, not that you'd want to breathe anyway, because your lungs would literally roll up in protest like one of those kids' birthday party blowers. You do what you have to do, but you're getting dizzy now, and starting to lose consciousness from lack of air, and then, darkness envelops you.

You stumble out of the wretched chamber and gasp in as many large gulps of fresh air as you can force into your lungs. The rest of the day is spent hanging out with hundreds of other band and crew guys who all look exactly alike because we all dress the same, like mutant postapocalyptic gas station attendants with wallet chains, tattoos, and baseball hats, and so, of course, when you say, "What's up?" to each other you can't remember their names and they think you're a stuck-up asshole when in reality you're just getting old and senile from too many beers and barbecues and music pounding into your head all day and so then you start walking around checking out other bands you've seen play so many times already you know exactly what they are going to say in between songs before they even know it themselves, and it's going to be things like, "How's everybody doing? Hey, Warped Tour, you guys having a good time? Let's hear some noise! What's up, Chicago!?! We want to see you guys go off to this one! This is off our new album! Are you guys having a good time?"

Finally it's time to play the show, and you argue with your band members about what songs you are going to play and you see Big Mitch, the head of security, and you say, "It's hot," and he says, "Yep, it's fucking hot," and then you go on stage and the crowd roars and you sweat and strain and freak out and forget the words to the fourth song and then you get hit in the head with a shoe and you scream at the crowd about this fucked-up world we live in, the perfect people looking down on you, and corrupt governments, greedy corporations, and hypocritical religious fanatics trying to rip off and exploit the working class and you generally have a great time rallying against the futility of it all and you stage dive and the crowd goes nuts and everyone's feeling good and you play your last song and come off the stage feeling drained and exhausted and soaking wet with sweat and you collapse somewhere and before you know it someone will be firing up the barbecue and handing you a beer and you'll be ready to do it all over again.

You come home after a month and a half of doing this day after day and your liver will be shot, you'll have a scorching case of athlete's foot, your brain will feel like a soggy sponge, and you will absolutely detest every pore and skin particle of your band members and crew, but at the same time you love every one of them like a brother with whom you survived a plane crash in the Himalayas, and you'll wonder how you possibly made it through without having a catastrophic mental and emotional breakdown.

When you get home and you're ready to fall onto the couch and not get up for several days, your wife will be so tired from taking care of the kids while you were gone, she'll just hand them over to you when you walk in the door and then keep on walking.

PUNK ROCK ERRAND BOY

Since my wife had the breastfeeding boobs and stayed home and did most of the work with the baby while I was on tour, my job when I was home usually became running errands and picking up groceries and baby supplies and the prescriptions she'd need filled when the little germ receptacles would get a cold, fever, or become constipated. Jennifer takes perverse pleasure in sending me to the store to get the items that cause most men extreme embarrassment to bring to the check-out counter. There is nipple cream; breast pads; maxi, mini, and supermaxi pads with wings; and all kinds of other strange apparatus she needs me to buy and take the heat for at the cash register. Also, for some reason, many of the products the kids require are anally related, from anal suppositories and rectal thermometers to all varieties of diaper rash powders and ointments, which are equally embarrassing to inquire about.

Once I was sent on a mission to the nearest Drug Emporium to retrieve all kinds of ointments, salves, and snake oils when the baby had a fever. Once again I was given a list by my wife of intricate detail of the exact brand she wanted, with product specifications and age requirements for each item, because obviously I am not to be trusted to know the difference between Tylenol for Kids, Advil Sinus Jr., Pediatric Liquid Ibuprofen, and St. Joseph's Baby Aspirin Horse Tranquilizers for Toddlers between ages two and five that are stacked up six shelves high on the baby aisle. These are all child versions of the adult products, and you know this because the kid version has a picture of a purple dinosaur or a friendly giraffe right next to the warning sign that says if you give so much as one milligram more than the recommended amount to your infant, you'll send them into epileptic shock. In the aisle with you there will be about four other dads with bed head who'll be looking at their lists and scanning the football field-long aisle of baby medicine with a "What the fuck?" look on their face just like yours.

So after literally an hour of searching to find the exact right kind of medicines, I go over to the men's aisle to acquire the phalanx of toiletries a middle-aged punk rock dad needs to fool his teenage fans into thinking he's closer to their age than their old man's. I throw my booty into the cart, thinking I'm probably going to have to take out a second mortgage to pay for all the products I need to keep my baby healthy and let me pretend I'm twenty a little longer.

I bring everything up to the register and empty it all out and notice the guy working is an eighteen-year-old-looking dude with sideburns, dyed black hair, hand tattoos, and an eyebrow ring, the exact Pennywise demographic. Because I am the epitome of the local celebrity, I'm hardly ever recognized in public, mainly due to the fact that our band has never risen above cult status, the apex of our career being when we were featured on *Access Hollywood* because Pat O'Brien's twelve-year-old kid was a fan, but also because I'm completely in-distinguishable from the millions of other goateed, baseball cap-wearing surf-skate/action sports/extreme this and that punk guys driving next to you on the freeway in a 4x4 with multiple large motocross decals on the tinted back window. Very often I'll see someone staring at me and think I'm being recognized and act all cool like I'm being hounded for auto-graphs, but instead they just think I'm their buddy Steve. If this checkout guy does recognize me, he'd have to be a hard-core fan to be able to distinguish me from any of the other five hundred extreme action sports guys who walk through his aisle every day.

"Hey, aren't you the guy from Pennywise?"

At the same time I get a shot of adrenaline from the ego boost, I think about what's on the conveyor belt in front of me.

"Yeah, what's up?"

"Dude, I used to listen to you guys when I was a kid."

"What, when you were two?"

He starts saying "rad" a lot, like I do, and wants me to sign something for him, and then says his friend Paul loves us and he won't believe this, and asks another few questions before he remembers he's actually working and starts to scan my items through. With each item, he and I are both let down further and further. Children's anal suppository. Child rectal thermometer. Diaper rash cream. Breast pads. Just for Men Extra Gray Coverage Brown Hair Dye. Metamucil. Nair for Men. Mylanta. With each swipe across the scanner I go from being punk rock, superstar, Warped Tour legend, to rapidly aging, grayhaired father of a constipated child, with a nipple-dripping wife. I'm not a radical, punk-scene voice of a generation, I'm a pathetic middle-aged loser having problems with heartburn, irregularity, and back hair.

"That'll be $95.10."

I hand him the cash and sulk away. I envision him tossing out the paper he had me sign and the band losing one more unit of sales all because the checkout guy saw me at my weakest moment.

This is all part of the game of being a parent. When I signed up to be a dad I had to leave my cool and my self-respect at the maternity room doors. On our white minivan we have no less than three life-size decals of Britney Spears's face stuck to the windows. A friend saw me driving the wife and kids in it and said he was going to the record store to trade in all his Pennywise records. I told him to get me the new Christina Aguilera while he was there because the kids were begging me for it.

4

MOMMY'S LITTLE
MONSTER

Kids figure out at an early age what's cool and what sucks. Chocolate, candy, gum, TV, toys, games, and bikes are cool; flu shots, vegetables, taking medicine, and going to the dentist suck. They like to play dress up and put on thousands of different costumes in a given day, but they hate putting on real clothes to go out to dinner or wearing a jacket when it's cold. My girls will put pajamas on their dolly and brush dolly's teeth and comb dolly's hair and put dolly into her little dolly bunk bed, but just try getting them to do it for themselves in less than five hours without having to threaten to cancel all their play dates for a year, it won't happen.

Our kids always became very strong-willed and independent at an age we were never really prepared for. It amazes me how a person an eighth of my size can dictate what, when, and how I do things and basically control my entire life. They become so defiant to your will you'll wonder if you'll ever be able to get them to do anything they don't want to do. She doesn't want the bowl of cereal you just poured for her, she wants waffles. He wants to wear the blue shirt with the Superman sign, not the red striped one with the football. No, she won't take the cough medicine you drove through the rain to get for her, it tastes yucky. He doesn't want to go to school, he wants to stay home and eat ice cream and watch cartoons all day.

Deep inside, we are proud of this independent spirit. It should remind us of when we were little punks and wanted to stand up to the man and do things our own way. But that all flies out the window when you're late for a doctor's appointment and the four-year-old won't get in the car or put on pants and is now streaking down the sidewalk bottomless. An independent spirit is great as a concept, but not as good when your kid is running around your neighborhood without pants on.

Almost exactly to the day when my kids had their second birthdays, they started acting different. They verbalize their requests, so instead of just crying to get what they want, they have this crying/talking/moaning thing they do called whining. Whining operates at a decibel level that is so annoying to a man's eardrum follicles that he'll immediately do anything to get it to stop, throwing all advice to the contrary out the window. Our children figured this out early on and would employ the whining tactic to get anything from chocolate milk and French fries for breakfast to whatever overpriced toy they wanted at the toy store. I'm still amazed when I'm sitting next to my kid at midnight on the couch watching TV because they whined so convincingly to "please let me stay for five more minutes, *pleeeeease!*" (While I'm writing this, my two-year-old has been coming in and out of the room with different nude

Barbie dolls, whining, crying, and demanding that I somehow fit the stretch pants made for the tiny Polly Pocket doll onto Cinderella Barbie, who is a good three inches taller, and she cries huge heavy tears when I can't get them to fit. From my friends with boys, I hear they're just as bad, if not worse.)

Daughter number three has just recently learned she has the power to use the word "No." "No," she doesn't want to take a bath, "No," she doesn't want lunch, "No," she won't brush her teeth, and "No," she doesn't want to be a good girl and please do what Daddy says before he has a nervous breakdown. She's also perfected the art of the Oscar Award–winning tantrum, with requisite back arch, air kicks, breath holding while screaming at the same time, and turning colors. With whining, tantrums, and "no," I found myself in all kinds of embarrassing situations where I had to either cave in and give them what they wanted, or curl up in a ball and cry. These years are known as the Terrible Twos, and they usually last well into high school.

Although if I'd have to choose a great time to be both a parent and a kid, it's the toddler years. They can be the most challenging times, but they're also the most fun. Toddlers have all their emotions right there on the surface. They haven't learned yet to be fake and subvert what they really think and feel in life. They let everyone in the room know emphatically what they want, what they're scared of, and when they have to go number two. Wouldn't it be nice if you could just walk into your boss's office and whine that you really want a big raise and then throw yourself on the carpet, hold your breath, and arch your back if he doesn't give you one? At a company luncheon, during a speech, you could just grab your pee-pee and do a little dance and everyone would know you had to go to the bathroom. Later on, we slowly learn that to function in society we need to suppress and hide our darkest fears and deepest desires, which makes sense, I guess, because you wouldn't want to tell your best friend that deep inside you're scared to death of growing old and dying and that you would really love to have sex with his wife. When you're a kid, you tell it like it is and never spare the details.

Why do we like toddlers so much when they can be such a struggle to deal with? First of all, they're just cute as hell. They have none of the repulsive things that come with age; wrinkles, acne, liver spots, back hair, etc. Secondly, their whole existence is about having fun. They just wander around the house looking for things to play with or fun things to explore, and they can get hours of enjoyment out of everyday household objects like a broom or a toilet paper roll. They don't know anything about war or poverty or death or any of the things that keep us up all night worrying. Imagine if we intelligent adults could keep this mind-set throughout our entire lives. Instead of wanting to go to war with Russia, we would call them up and ask them if they wanted to come over and play instead.

As much fun as the toddler is, though, they can be equally, catastrophically frustrating, to the point that it drives me into the garage looking for the hidden pack of cigarettes I don't smoke anymore. This is the beginning of a child's sense of independence when they begin establishing their will to do things their own way, and, like adults, they can become drunk with power. You're proud when your kid says, "I do it," the first time they want to open the door themselves or pull up their own trousers, but less so when, from that point on, they insist on pouring their own milk all over the table, buttoning each of the six hundred buttons on their jacket, and taking three hundred years to climb into the car seat and buckle themselves in when you're in a hurry. I tried to look at these as important growth skills they were developing, and not devious tactics Satan had given them to mess with my head, so I could save my brain and liver a lot of trouble.

I'M GOING FOR A WALK

When our kids were around a year old and had been crawling around on the floor on hands and knees and gingerly pulling themselves up onto coffee tables, of course we started to wonder when they were going to take their first steps. Invariably this was when some a-hole parent would come over with their one-year-old who was walking already and say, "Oh, your little one isn't walking yet? My little Johnny has been walking since he was six months old. I guess some kids aren't as advanced as others. I'm sure your little one won't be crawling around on all fours like a barnyard animal forever." Did I mention yet that other parents suck?

After going through it with daughter number one, we were never in a huge hurry for our kids to take their first steps, because when they do start walking it's about one hundred times harder to keep track of them, and walking leads to climbing and falling, and you'll never be able to take your eye off them again for the next several years. When they are only crawling, you can rest assured they aren't going to walk over to the stove, reach up, and grab the pot of boiling water or flip on the wall heater because they can't reach anything too dangerous yet. You also don't have to worry they're going to open the front door and walk out into oncoming traffic.

Once our kids finally did get up the nerve to try taking a few steps on their own, it opened up a whole new world for them, and a whole new can of headaches for us, but it's great seeing their obvious pride at their accomplishment. On the night in our tiny living room when a toddling daughter number one released herself from her mom's clutches and took her first few shakily balanced steps toward me across the carpet, with an ear-to-ear grin on her face, it was like meeting her for the first time all over again. Kids are somewhat prehuman until they are bipedaling around like the rest of us, and they must sense that groveling around on the floor makes them less than a full-fledged citizen of the household. Daughter number one had this new sense of pride and was soon spending most of her time roaming around the house all self-assured and cocky, looking at all the areas she couldn't see as lowly floor dweller.

Kid-proofing your house is an ongoing task for parents and probably ends with you securing the liquor cabinet when they're teenagers and moving all your savings into offshore accounts when they're looking to buy a house. My kids' new ambulatory state meant that we needed to keep the house picked up a little more from our usual state of chaos and triple-check all the dangerous areas where they could get into trouble. New walkers don't just go from crawling on the carpet to strutting like a runway model overnight. They're always about one wobble away from a face plant. There were months and months of cartwheeling spills, tumbling falls, and gravity-defying backflips, so keeping their walking area as free from toy debris as possible and padding the sharp edges of the furniture went a long way in reducing our emergency room bill.

"LEARNED TO WALK WHILE I WAS AWAY"

When we're out on the road doing our own shows, there's not much to do all day before the show, so instead of hanging around the venue at sound check and listening to the drum tech pound the kick drum over and over until the constant pounding becomes a constant pounding in my head, or being tortured by Fletcher plucking out poorly played renditions of "Crazy Train" and "Enter Sandman," at earsplitting volume as he tweaks his guitar sound, trying every conceivable variation of distortion only to end up using the exact same settings he uses every night, I like to take a walk around and check out the sights of whatever city we're in. I usually just wander around and try to pick out a cheap toy or "Hard Rock Amsterdam" T-shirt for the kids and take pictures of anything stupid I see. It doesn't take long to figure out that this is just another dumb city with the same dumb stores, and no matter where you are on the planet, downtown there's always a Starbucks, a Subway, and a McDonald's, then a jewelry store, an arcade, a strip club, a few clothing stores, and, of course, the tourist trap store with postcards and beach towels and rubber sandals and ceramic pineapple ashtrays, and walking around in circles for two hours, I find that the succession of these desperate establishments just repeats itself over and over until I start to feel slightly nauseous.

I get back to the hotel and see the pamphlets in the lobby for all the fun things I should be doing in the city. *Ride the rapids in an inflatable boat! Take a tram up to the mountaintop for fabulous views of the city! Careen around the lake on a hovercraft! Visit the wax museum! Rent a convertible Jeep and tour the area looking like a total asshole!* All these things would take time and effort and money and waiting in lines and cab rides and interacting with humanity, and I consider for a second if the one minute of ex-hilaration would be worth the investment of time and money as I'm pushing the elevator button to my floor to go lay down and watch *Oprah* dubbed into German.

Eventually I call my wife at home and even though it's midday for me, it's bed time for them and she tells me I missed quite a lot today. Daughter number two had a soccer game and scored all three goals for her team, and afterward, when my wife asked her if she was proud of herself she said, "Yeah, but I wish Daddy was here to see it." Even better, though, after the game they were in the living room and number three took her first few steps unassisted! Instantly the words to that old Harry Chapin song, "... learned to walk while I was away," started echoing in my head, about a guy being too busy with work and missing out on his kids' childhood. I used to listen to the song over and over as a kid myself when my own dad was off on business and missed one of my little league games, and while Jennifer's talking about how great it was and how proud she was of herself walking across the room for the first time, the lyrics keep repeating in my head, until my heart sinks like a heavy rock into my stomach and doesn't leave there for the rest of the day.

Then the oldest daughter picks up the phone and she's read-ing a book but she says that her sister kicked her today, but in the background number two screams that "SHE SCRATCHED ME FIRST!" and then number one says, "DID NOT," and then they repeat "DID NOT!" "DID TOO!" "DID NOT!" "DID TOO!" "DID NOT!" "DID TOO!" about fifty times. I coax her back onto the phone and remind her of our deal that if they get along real good for Mommy while I'm gone, I'll take them to Disneyland or Lego Land or something with a land on the end of it when I get back, but if they fight a lot, well, then I'll just take the toys I bought them while I've been traveling and give them to some orphan kids. They both scream, "NO!" and promise me they'll be good and won't fight. I ask where Mom is and they say she's unloading the dryer or the dishwasher and then say the little one really wants to talk to me, and she grabs the phone and starts saying, "Da-da, Da-da" into the listening end and then her voice kind of trails off as something else catches her eye and she forgets that I'm on the phone and just drops it on the carpet and wanders off somewhere. I sit on the carpet for a while and listen to her talking to her Barbies and note that the older two have stopped fighting and I can hear they're watching *That's So Raven* in the background. From ten thousand miles away I close my eyes and pretend I'm sitting in the room with them and try to see if I can telepathically materialize myself home like in *Star Trek*, but after a while I open them and look around and I'm still in the crappy hotel room watching *Oprah* and wondering what the hell I'm doing here.

Later on that day I have to do a radio interview with some young asshole scenester guy in perfectly unkempt thrift store clothes, mod hair, and unironic 1970s sideburns, who keeps commenting about how "the band has been at it a long time," and that "we're still going," and that "we've "been around for years," and while he's talking, I start to wonder if Picasso, when he entered his blue period, had to endure some smug, indie-scene guy in corduroy pants continually making note of the fact that he didn't just pick up a paintbrush for the first time yesterday. He gets all the information about the band wrong, saying we have a new album out when it actually came out a year and a half ago, he gives the wrong tour dates, calls the song of ours he played by the wrong name, and then says unapologetically that he's not familiar with our music, really, and that someone else was supposed to do the interview and that he's just filling in. You can tell he desperately wishes he was interviewing the latest trendy male-model-poster-boy band of the month in their vintage clothes that he dresses exactly like and who play watered-down versions of U2, the Cure, and Gang of Four, and have a big hit on the radio today, but will be completely forgotten a year from now. When he asks me for the twelfth time what it's like still being up there playing at the Warped Tour ten years later, I stifle the urge to scream, "LOOK, I JUST MISSED SEEING MY ONE-YEAR-OLD TAKE HER FIRST STEPS AND MY FIVE-YEAR-OLD SCORE THREE GOALS AT HER SOCCER GAME, AND NOW I'VE GOT THIS *CAT'S IN THE CRADLE*" SONG PLAYING IN MY HEAD ALL DAY, SO I REALLY COULDN'T GIVE ONE SMALL, DEEP-FRIED TURD ABOUT YOUR GOD DAMNED RADIO SHOW AND YOUR STUPID INDIE HAIR-CUT!"

Instead, I smile politely and answer the question that yes, it is amazing that we're still playing after all these years, and no, we won't change our style to keep up with the latest trends on the radio because wouldn't that be like asking Muddy Waters to stop playing the blues or Pavarotti to stop singing operas, and yes, the shows have been going well, and no, we don't have anything new planned for the show tonight, and yes, I do have a few final words to say to our fans in Belgium. "Never give up hope, and always be there for your kids' soccer games!"

SMALL MAN, BIG MOUTH

As soon as we were done worrying about when our kids were going to walk like everyone else, then we started worrying about when they were going to talk like everyone else. They start making all kinds of gurgling sounds and various noises from an early age, but once we started reading books to them at night, they started mimicking the sounds we were making and pointing to things and saying, "Whusssat?" From then on, our home became one big speech-training class with us teaching them new words every day just by talking to them, instructing them on the right way to pronounce things, and carrying on mindless conversations with them about "Why is purple?"

The two-year-old is still learning her way around the grammatical inflections of the English language, and during a quiet interlude at a recent third-grade symphony recital, when we sat in the cramped bleachers at the high school gymnasium with hundreds of other sweating parents, she shouted out, "DADDY, MY JUST FARTED!" I tried to quiet her but she insists I acknowledge her accomplishment. "DADDY! DADDY! MY JUST FARTED!! MY JUST FARTED!!" Another time she was padding around with no clothes on after a bath when a sock became lodged in her gluteal crevice. Her older sisters screamed in delight, "Look at her butt-crack!" We all laughed hysterically at the sight of the little sock dangling like a tail behind her. She then deduced that anytime you needed a good laugh, you just need to yell, "Butt-crack," and everyone would love it. This proved problematic when at grocery stores she would respond to checkers who asked her name by replying, "Butt-crack!" or when our two elderly neighbors walked away down the sidewalk after a polite evening conversation, she called out after them, "BYE-BYE, BUTT-CRACKS!"

It takes so long for them to start stringing actual sentences together you may become convinced your child has a speech problem. Daughter number one stuttered when she was about three years old like a motor that wouldn't start. "Wha-wha-wha-wha-wha-wha-wha-wha-wha-what is that, Mommy?" We, of course, made a big deal about it and worried that she'd never grow out of it, but after a few months, it eventually went away. Daughter number three started doing it and we ignored it and it was gone within a week. Daughter number two, however, had a lot of earaches as a child and had to have tubes put in her ears, which affected her hearing and speech. She said "geel" for "girl" and had trouble with her R's and L's as if she was a little native Japanese person. Eventually, after a few sessions with the speech therapist, the problem was resolved and we never had to have a Cindy Brady episode where I had to hire a five-year-old hit man to beat up the kid who was teasing my kids about talking baby talk.

We tried not to let our kids' peculiar speech issues bother us unless the problem didn't correct itself or seemed like it needed expert attention. Our kids were soon talking incessantly, especially in the seven- to nine-year-old range when they rarely, if ever, stop jabbering away nonsensically and singing strange songs and gossiping and complaining and teasing and whining and are just basically going on and on about anything until I have a dull ache between my ears from all the constant blabbering. Now I wonder why I ever worried about them talking at all.

POTTY TRAINING

I define becoming a toddler as when your kid is walking and talking, but some people might include taking a crap in a toilet instead of in a cloth in between their legs in that definition. Getting your child to go from someone who relieves themselves while sitting on your living room couch to someone who does it while sitting on a commode can either be a simple process or one that takes months of torment. We started the girls on the potty training train by trying to get them to agree how gross and smelly and yucky it is to have a diaper full of warm dung between their legs and then casually mentioned that people were starting to talk behind their back about it.

What usually caused me to exclaim in a loud voice to my wife that "POTTY TRAINING BEGINS NOW" was an episode that happened to varying degrees with all three of my children in my experience as a diaper changer. I would be changing the kids' fully loaded diaper like any other time, but suddenly, before I could scream, "NO!" they'd reach down and sink their hands knuckles-deep down into the mess between their legs. My fight-or-flight reflexes won't allow me to wait the time it would take to find an appropriate cloth or baby wipe to get rid of it, so I'll wipe it on my shirt or the baby clothes or the changing pad sheet or anything within reaching distance. Within the space of five seconds everything around me, myself, the baby, most of both of our clothing, and all the furniture, will have a dollop of fresh poo on it. It's never about when the baby is ready to be potty trained, it's when you are.

Thus begins the messiest few weeks of your entire life. It will be a veritable shit storm. Once we made the huge mistake of trying to house-train a puppy while potty training a two-year-old, and walking in our family room was like following an equestrian parade down Main Street on New Year's Day. This is because pretty much the only way we've come up with to get a child to start using the toilet is to take away their diaper and tell them that now they get to wear "big kid" underwear. As much as they will be thrilled with this news, it will take several weeks of them standing there playing at their plastic kitchen with pee running down their leg to get them to realize they aren't wearing the diaper anymore.

The period of time when we were teaching our kids to use the toilet took a lot of patience just like everything else in parenting. Basically it was all about keeping a lot of industrial-strength carpet cleaner handy, and when an exploded diaper leaked all over my imitation leather car seat and seeped down into the seams and I had to have it professionally cleaned but the smell never completely went away, I tried to channel my frustration into an acceptable outlet that didn't become the biological equivalent of pounding my head against a brick wall. Before I knew it, they were potty trained and I didn't have to relive the drama of the two fistfuls of poo, at least until my next kid.

PEE BREAK

The toddler period is not surprisingly somewhat frightening for many kids. Adults are huge and can snatch you up at any time while you're playing with a toy, make scary faces at you, and then plop you back down at will. You get hurt a lot falling down and getting your fingers pinched in things and bonking your head everywhere you go. You pretty much never know when the next time you're going to get hurt or scared shitless is coming. Because of this, it's easy for them to develop a slight case of separation anxiety and entertain various irrational fears. We made the huge mistake of letting our two-year-old watch *Toy Story* before she was ready, and for years she was afraid that her dolls might suddenly animate and start talking to her in the middle of the night. Usually between the age of one and two, if my daughters couldn't find me or my wife, they'd have a total freak-out. Daughter number one would just follow my wife around the house with whatever toys she was playing with, going from kitchen, to living room, to bedroom, dragging her Barbie Fun House or life-size stuffed pony behind her.

In addition to being whip smart, well read, intelligent, and cute as a button, daughter number one has always been kind of fearful, somewhat jumpy, easily frightened, anxious in certain situations, scared of her own shadow, apprehensive in unfamiliar territory, terrified of everyday objects, anxious and worried about the unknown, and timid. I love this about her. She has your everyday kid fears of monsters in the closet, skeletons under the bed, and Bloody Marys in the mirror, but she also has irrational ones like being alone in a room and barfing. As a toddler, she was afraid of stretchy things that could snap like rubber bands, latex gloves, and balloons, and as an infant, if you sneezed when she wasn't expecting it, she would cry for hours.

I like people who have a healthy amount of skepticism and apprehension in life. They're realists. For every foolhardy, adventurous explorer with blind courage, constantly throwing caution to the wind, there should always be someone with a bit of common sense and hesitation saying, "Are you sure we should cross the steep gorge using the tattered, old rope bridge? Couldn't we just walk around?" I'm confident I won't have to worry about her doing any mountain climbing or bungee jumping when she gets older because she doesn't even like climbing to the top of the slide at the playground.

From a very young age, she also developed a pathological fear of toilets. She would never flush or want to be in the vicinity when someone hit the lever and the whirling torrent started whooshing down. When she was about three years old I asked her where her fear stemmed from and she said she saw a cartoon once where all the characters were sucked down into the toilet and down the drain. I guess to a small child the sloshing, spinning whirlpool devouring all its earthly contents could seem a little frightening, and I've heard of other kids who share this phobia. The problem was that she hadn't grown out of it by the time she was nearly four years old. She had no problem taking a pee in a toilet as long as you didn't flush it when she was in the vicinity, but when she had to go number two, she'd make us throw a pull-up diaper on her real quick so she could take care of business, standing there turning red leaning next to the toilet. Every parenting expert will say how embarrassingly indulgent this was and that we should have forced her to go number two on the potty years before, but it was our first kid, we let her do what she wanted. She could have demanded to do it into our hands and we probably would have obliged her. The problem was a pathological fear of toilets made peeing in certain public restrooms problematic.

I didn't realize just how bad it had gotten until one afternoon I took her to the mall to help her buy her mom a Mother's Day present. Ten minutes after getting there, she tells me she has to go to the bathroom. It seems it's not a problem for women to bring their little sons into women's restrooms because apparently these places are like luxury lounges with changing tables, tampon dispensers, and an on-call staff supplying everything a mother needs for mothering. On the other hand, men's rooms are kind of forbidding, desolate places. I don't really like bringing my daughter into the men's restroom, as we're not the most genteel creatures, and there's a good chance she could hear, see, or smell some things that could scar her for life.

So in order to find a private bathroom for her to do her business, I ducked into a Foot Locker and asked the sixteen-year-old referee behind the counter if we could use their bathroom. "Sorry, sir. We can't let customers use the restroom. It's for Foot Locker employees only."

I darted across to some type of beauty supply store where there was an older lady with tons of garish makeup smudged all over her face, gray roots beneath jet black hair, and bifocals, hovering over a teenage Latina girl working the counter, which was littered with all kinds of makeup swatches, lip gloss capsules, and eyeliner pencils, and the smell of the combined floral perfumes was suffocating. Even though they looked strange standing in their floral-scented beauty product boutique, they were both giving me a weird look. Being a musician in a skate punk band, and not someone with a nine-to-five job and no one to impress, when I'm not on tour I don't really worry much about my physical appearance. I rarely shower, I have about five days' growth worth of stubble, and never wash or comb my hair. I'm wearing the wrinkled shorts and shirt I slept in, I probably smell a little ripe, and I'm holding the hand of a small girl asking to use their bathroom. I suddenly realize this looks a little weird.

They reluctantly agree to let us use their facilities and in the tiny back storeroom littered with boxes of all kinds of mingling perfumes and makeups, I find an even tinier bathroom. For a beauty supply store selling products to improve your appearance and public image, they have sorely neglected their toilet, which is desperately in need of a makeover. There are rusty water stains, strange particles clinging to the bowl, and various curly black hairs draped over the rim.

Daughter number one takes one look it at and says, "Unh-unh. No way."

"Come on, pumpkin. Just hover over the rim. Daddy will hold you up and you won't even have to sit on the seat." I can tell by her expression, sad eyes, and crossed arms, she's not having it.

Now we're zigzagging across the mall to different stores and trying to find a bathroom, and she's complaining, "Daaadeeeee, I reeeeallly neeed to gooo noooowww!" I go to the Sam Goody Record Store and get the "Employees Only" response from the pimply faced teenage boy working the cash register. The new Marilyn Manson CD is blasting so loud on the speakers I can hardly hear him. I'm ready to leave but then hastily decide to do something I promise myself never to do. Drop the P-Bomb. This never works out well.

"Hey, do you like punk music?"

"Yeah, I-I guess." He too is looking at me a little weird, probably not used to having strange dudes with kids asking them about their taste in music at 11 A.M. on a Tuesday.

"Ever hear of Pennywise?"

"Huh?'

"You know, Epitaph Records? Rancid? The Offspring? NOFX?"

"We have Offspring's latest album on sale right now in aisle three."

"Yeah, but I'm in the band Pennywise. I'm the lead singer. Is there any way you could just cut me a break and let me use the bathroom so my kid can take a pee?"

"Oh, okay, uh. Well, um. No. My manager could be coming back any minute, and I just got this job and I don't want to get busted. And, uh, I'm kinda more into goth and rap."

What the fuck? Did I just get dissed by the Sam Goody kid? I can't believe this. I'm so desperate I'm dropping my band name and getting my ego shattered all because my kid is scared of toilets.

I yank her by the arm out of the store and leave the mini-Marilyn wanksta to his bad taste in music and we go next door to the luggage/wallet/expensive pen store run by two hairy Turkish-looking dudes. After explaining my situation to them twice, one says, "Vaht? She vahnt to juse deh choilet?" They talk in Turkish to each other for like five minutes and at this point my daughter is visibly holding herself, crossing her legs, and turning yellow. I yell out, "JUST LET ME USE THE GODDAMN BATHROOM! PLEASE!!"

The hairier one just points to the door to the back room.

I find the toilet inside the forest of cardboard boxes, and find it to be strangely immaculate. I can't help pondering for a moment why the bathroom of the two hairy Turkish dudes is so much cleaner than the ladies' room at the beauty supply store. Whatever.

She hikes her little dress up and appears ready to go, but then suddenly stops midsquat and says, "What's that sound?"

"What? Nothing. I don't hear anything."

"No, listen."

I don't hear anything at all. It's strangely quiet in there, the boxes of luggage surrounding the bathroom providing better sound absorption than some of the high-priced recording studios I'd been in. All I hear is the faint sound of the water lightly hissing in the toilet.

"The toilet's making noises."

Then I remember she can't stand it when an idle toilet is either leaky or filling back up with water slowly. It probably reminds her of a rattling cobra ready to strike and yank her by its porcelain fangs down into the sewer pipes to devour her.

"It's scaring me, I want a different toilet."

"Are you serious? You're not serious. You're serious. Oh, my God, I'm going to kill your mom." Whenever my kids have a mini-psychosis or irrational fear of any kind, it's always my wife's fault.

At some point we finally get to a camera store with a lady working who looks like she's someone's mom and she says of course we can use her bathroom, and my daughter asks her if it's a clean toilet that doesn't make weird sounds, and she says yes and she totally understands and that she didn't like scary toilets as a kid, either. I sigh a huge sigh of relief and it's great to at last be in the presence of someone sympathetic to my plight and when the pee finally comes, even though I'm not the one doing it, I get as much relief as if I'd held my own through extra innings at a ball game.

SOCIAL DISTORTION

Jennifer and I were at a Memorial Day/birthday backyard barbecue recently, and scattered around the grass, playing on the enormous redwood swing/slide/tree house and sliding down the giant rented blow-up slide, were toddlers and children of every shape, size, and color, running around screaming and playing and having your typical backyard party freak-out. After chowing down on hot dogs and hamburgers and birthday cake and ice cream, all were on a fevered sugar high. At times, the volume of the midget mayhem was enough to cause even someone who's had stacks of guitar amplifiers blowing distortion into his ears for the last decade to wince in pain. There were older boys play-fighting and swashbuckling with plastic swords and younger girls sneaking around and devising ways to embarrass each other by telling the boys one of them liked them, but there were also little wobbling towheaded toddlers playing in sandlots with buckets and shovels, clutching dolls and slurping away on sippy cups. My wife and I, seated in lawn chairs nearby, sipping margaritas and chatting with some of the other beleaguered parents, were shocked when right in front of us my normally sweet as pie two-year-old suddenly snatched back a doll she had been playing with from the hands of another little girl who'd innocently picked it up, and then when the offended party protested, she bashed her over the head with it three times and screamed in the horrified and slightly dazed child's face, *"NOOOO!! MIIIIINNNE!!"* We took her aside and tried to explain that she had to learn to share and she wasn't allowed to hit other people when they did things she didn't like. She just looked at us like we were either crazy or we'd had one too many margaritas because there's no way anyone's taking her favorite doll and not walking away with a few lumps.

Even though we knew about our children's social tendencies, as soon as they were walking and talking we knew we had to start letting them socialize with other kids their age. It's great at first when two little kids come up to each other and start talking gibberish and are all excited to see another person their same height standing in front of them. Unfortunately, the cuteness only lasts a couple of seconds as soon as one figures out that the other has something they want or finds them sitting on their favorite swing. This was not the time to leave them unattended and let them work things out for themselves because usually it came to painful baby blows and someone would toddle away from the altercation missing a small fistful of hair. At this early stage in their lives, if things go right they can build a lifelong friendship that will provide them with years of cherished memories; if they go wrong, the paramedics could be called and someone could be brought up on charges.

BOTTLED VIOLENCE

People are violent. We all have the urge to strangle someone at one point or another, and when I used to have to drive home from work on the 405 every day, I would have that urge several times a day. There are a few people that if I could get away with it, like if God and the cops were distracted somehow, I swear I could rip that person's eyeballs right out of their skull. It's okay to feel this way from time to time. People piss you off. It's natural. Luckily, we're all civilized human beings and we know that acting on our violent impulses is morally wrong. Right after you entertain the thought of ripping someone's eyeballs out, you come to your senses and realize it's not nice to hurt someone else just because they make you mad, but more importantly, even if you would enjoy doing it, becoming Ms. Prison Cell Mate of the Month sucks really bad.

Unfortunately, little kids don't realize they aren't supposed to act on their violent impulses. The problem becomes that the person being punched, kicked, or bitten isn't going to like it very much, and neither are their parents, especially the father. I know when my kids get hit, bit, or kicked by someone it takes a long time to convince myself not to get in the car and go over to the perpetrator's house and beat the crap out of the father of the household on their front lawn.

We had to be extra vigilant when we had a known biter or hitter over for a play date. For some reason, many of the biter parents are oblivious to the whole thing or act like it's not a big deal and do little to try to stop it. We know one parent who, when his kid hits or bites, just says, "What can I do? He's two." Once again, either he is a complete moron or can't recognize this as extremely inconsiderate behavior. It's never too early to start instructing kids on the proper way to act and the meaning of the word "No!" with a raised finger in their face, just not the middle one. I don't know why parents can teach their kids not to do things like walk out into traffic, but can't figure out that you should probably tell them not to hit or bite other kids. It's called being a parent, look into it. How would you like it if I came up and took a bite out of your shoulder? You'd like it a lot less if I did it and then my wife said, "What can I do? He's forty!"

I've never told another parent how to raise his or her kids, because I'm surely no expert. I don't think anyone is. Even the Dr. Spock guy probably had plenty of issues with his kids or else he wouldn't have known how to write a book about it. But I do know what common sense is, and most of the time, how not to be an a-hole. Some situations are impossible to avoid, but there are plenty that are easy to, as long as you obey the golden rule of "Don't be an asshole unto others." If you don't want your kid getting sick all the time, don't bring your sick kid to play dates, and if you don't want your kid coming home with a hole bitten out of his arm, teach them not to hit or bite.

There were other social gatherings where daughter number one would go to a birthday party or event and be so shy she'd just stand behind us and cling to our legs, and anytime the well-meaning hostess or another child would come up and offer her a toy to play with or piece of cake to try and draw her out into the party, she would bury her head in our cargo pants and cry. I have no idea why being in someone's backyard surrounded by friends and toys and piñatas would cause such extreme social embarrassment, but apparently it did. We'd make excuses for her and say she'd just woken up from a nap or that she was coming down with something, so that the shunned party giver wouldn't feel offended, and this way we also didn't have to admit that our child had inherited some of the extreme social anxiety we'd both suffered through as kids.

Kids come in all different varieties of temperaments. Some are confident and social and outgoing, while others are a little more shy and cautious. Some like to read books quietly in the corner while others like to climb trees and throw rocks at cars. My kids are all over the temperament map, so I have to encourage the shyer one to be a little more outgoing to make new friends, and then try to restrain the aggro one from beaning their play-date in the melon with whatever ball she happens to be playing with. Daughter number two has never had much of a problem at social gatherings and is usually the first to want to demonstrate her skills at swingset gymnastics and kicking your favorite soccer ball into your neighbor's yard, but there were times in kindergarten when she couldn't find anyone to sit next to at lunch and worried so much about it the night before she'd keep herself up with a stomachache. Just when I thought I had escaped the social pressures of high school, college, and dating, I had to go through it all again with my kids, standing and turning red in the face when they wouldn't join the party, or worse, when they dented some kid's skull with a Cabbage Patch doll.

We try to impress upon our kids when we send them over to someone else's house on a play date that they need to be on their best behavior, that they try to remember to say "please" and "thank you" a lot, and that they play by the other family's rules if they want to be invited back. Daughter number one has a strange habit at sleepovers of attempting to bond with the family she's visiting by divulging our deep dark family secrets. One mom dropped her off in the morning and said she'd whispered to them that "sometimes my daddy smokes cigarettes in the garage, but we're not supposed to know," and then another mom called to tell us that when they tucked her in the night before, she'd confided that "my daddy farts in his sleep." Jennifer had said this jokingly once when I commented that she talked in her sleep and apparently my six-year-old took it as fact. Although she's snuck into our bed in the middle of the night often enough to be an authority on the subject.

When you have a kid over to your house for a play date you are responsible for someone else's pride and joy. Full disclosure to their parents of everything that went on when they come to pick them up is mandatory because you don't want a situation where the kid says something confusing to their parents that makes you look bad. One time my oldest daughter had a friend over for the night and I was in our bedroom watching *The Sopranos*. When they eventually burst into the room, I told them the show I was watching was only for adults. The girl went home and told her parents that while they played I was in my room watching adult films.

GIMME, GIMME, GIMME

So your buddy comes over and wants to borrow your limited-edition, import, green vinyl Misfits *Walk Among Us* album and you immediately start cataloging in your mind all the things he's borrowed over the years and traded for pot money or given back to you in an extremely altered condition, usually involving cat urine stains of some kind. You make up an excuse saying that your little sister wanted to borrow it for a science project about the resiliency of plastic mediums, but he knows you're full of shit and doesn't invite you to his next party for being a selfish a-hole and not parting with your precious Misfits import, you materialistic pig!

Imagine, then, if you are two years old and you have a Floppy Moppy doll you've slept with every night, drooled on, wiped your tears and nose with, cuddled against when you were scared or lonely, dragged around the house, and even slapped and beat in some bizarre acting out of a fight your parents once had. Then one day your mom brings a friend over who drops her little brat in front of you who's wearing a helmet to reshape his head and has bubbly green snot pouring out his nose. He sees you clutching your one true prized possession and could care less about your shiny new fire engine or Hot Wheels track; he wants Floppy

Moppy now! He tries to grab it from you, and when you recoil in horror, he flops back on the ground and throws a violent, convincing tantrum. Your mom rips Floppy from your clutches, hands it to Helmet Boy, points a finger at you, and says, "You need to learn how to 'share.'"

Kids hate sharing and so do we. They will readily share anything they don't care about: green beans, old socks, toys they've already played with a million times, but when it comes to things they really love or want to keep for themselves, being forced to hand it over to someone else seems like the ultimate betrayal. "Wait a minute. You gave birth to me, you clothe and feed me and put a roof over my head, but the first little moron that comes in off the street you hand over my Floppy Moppy? The betrayal! What kind of freakish Jekyll and Hyde parent are you?" Whenever I force my kids to share they look at me like I'm asking them to cut off a limb. Sharing is overrated in my book. It rarely works before the age of two or three, and after that, it's only done grudgingly. Kids know that sharing sucks and they make no secret of hating it. In fact, my kids love to gloat and flaunt in their siblings' faces the stick of gum or new toy they got that they don't have to share with them. So when I tell them they have to share it feels like I'm asking them to pull out all their teeth. It doesn't really seem fair. In fact, to them, it's extremely terrible.

I can't tell you how many times I scoured the F.A.O. Schwartz store in New York or the Toys "R" Us in Torrance searching for the perfect birthday toy for each child, or ducked into the candy store at Disneyland to get one of those huge spiral suckers that are bigger than your head, or stayed up late putting together a dolly baby stroller that was harder to assemble than a real one, and then present these hard-won riches to my children hoping for the abundant praise I so heartily deserved, only to have them reject the gift because they like what their sister got better. "Well, can't you two share?" I say meekly. Then the tears come. "How could you give her the exact thing that I wanted?" is what each heavy tear says. "Do you love her that much more?" Expecting effusive joy and thanks for my hard work, instead, I'm a heartless traitor. This is some of the hair-pulling-out frustration I spoke of earlier, and to deal with it I usually just throw my hands in the air, mumble that I can't win, and go in the garage and play angry Black Flag songs for about an hour.

This brings up another point. There is very little middle ground for kids. Either you're the greatest dad ever, hero of the world, can-do-no-wrong father of the decade, or you are the most loathsome, detestable let-down of a dad that's every darkened the corners of a playroom, and you can ping-pong back and forth between these extremes within a single conversation. There have been thousands of episodes in our parenting experience where I thought I was doing a great job only to find in their eyes that I couldn't have betrayed their trust more deviously if I had thrown all their favorite toys in a tree shredder.

Kids know that sharing sucks and they make no secret of hating it. When you're home alone the siblings know what's theirs and what isn't, but bring friends or neighbor kids into the equation and things get fuzzy. Their friends aren't going to sit there with nothing to play with, but which ones are your kids willing to share and which will they guard like the Holy Grail? It's hard to tell, but if you can't figure it out, the conflicts of sharing can make the best friendships go south, because the kids won't be able to get along, or worse, they'll start beating each other over the head with their Tonka trucks.

To help avoid embarrassing situations and keep the peace, we started hiding the select few toys that we knew our kids would go ballistic over if some little turd cames over and so much as breathed in the same air space as their Buzz Lightyear action figure. We discussed in advance what they're willing to share with friends and what needs to be locked away and hermetically sealed from play date invaders. Another more expensive option is buying two of the same toys for siblings who you know may be extremely jealous if one gets the Life-size Barbie and the other doesn't, which was how our Christmas was ruined one year. Even with all your advance work, there will still be times when you will have a huge sharing issue at some birthday party and you'll probably have to drag your kid screaming out of the house and all your friends will think you're a terrible parent so go ahead and start planning for that now.

RULES MADE UP BY YOU!

> "My daughter doesn't seem to feel that same need to rebel the way I did. She does well with whatever rules are applied to her. I think my son is gonna be the one who has problems there. At least with the rules we set around the house, he's not too good with following them. With my daughter it wasn't such a big deal because we never had to set many rules for her, but with my son he'll be the one with the hard time following authority."
>
> Noodles—*The Offspring*

Kids misbehave. Sometimes because they want something so badly they're willing to risk punishment and bodily injury to get it. Kids don't just want things, they "reeeeaaallllyyy, reeeealll-lyyy, please Dad, pleeeeeaaase Dad, I'll do aaaaaanything" want things. Other times they are just so spastically full of energy and impulsive they can't help themselves from kicking a soccer ball as hard as they can in the dining room. They have a hair-trigger time period between thinking of something naughty and fun to do and then realizing it's not a good idea. If you can't somehow get in between that split second of them coming up with the idea of writing "Daddy is a butt-head" in ink-pen on the living room wall, and them carrying out their plan, there will be nothing to stop them.

Growing up punk and disorderly, I don't have a hard time re-membering how easy it was to get into trouble, but now I'm in the odd position of having to teach my kids how to behave so I'm not constantly having to go down to the principal's office to bail them out. There are thousands of books, and now even TV shows, on how to discipline and deal with unruly kids, each one of them championing their own self-righteous, foolproof techniques on how to whip a strong-willed, impulsive kid into shape, with all kinds of cute catch phrases and admonitions for you to take charge of the situation and not let your three-year-old control you, like this is the easiest thing in the world, if you just follow their patented three-step plan.

For all the seminars I've been to on the subject, and all the TV shows and books I've seen and read, none of them have ever given me any real, definitive, concrete instructions on what to do when your kid is having a total conniption fit in the middle of a Wal-Mart, or going completely postal on you at the tot lot. They all deal with it in this vague, esoteric way, explaining that you need to show your child who's boss and administer positive discipline, and tell the child that it's not them but their behavior you don't like, but how does telling them this stop your four-year-old from yanking two fistfuls of hair out of the girl's head who just sat on his favorite swing at the park? Trust me, it doesn't. They'll look at you and say, "I'm glad you love me so much, now I'm going to drag this little girl over to the merry-go-round by her ponytails."

One of the great things about punk rock was that there weren't any rules on how it should be done. You were supposed to be able to dress, act, and play music any way you wanted, that was the beauty of it. Unfortunately it wasn't long before some punker-than-thou keepers of the flame started trying to define exactly what was, and wasn't punk, according to their own self-righteous criteria. Rules tell you what to do, and no self-respecting punk rocker likes to be told what to do. It's the same with parenting. Most of the rules from parenting guides on how to deal with unruly kids are so black and white they don't make room for shades of gray, and since every child is different, how could any one rule apply to everyone? Instead, there are principles. Principles describe basic ways of doing things that have worked in the past, and let you bend them for your own particular circumstances. From our experiences, nothing works all the time, but there are some concepts we've adopted that at least give the appearance that we know what we're doing.

I believe the most important principle to remember in being a parent and managing an unruly kid is first trying to lead by example. Kids usually mimic the mannerisms of their parents, so if you don't want your kid putting his feet up on the table and burping out the alphabet at dinnertime, don't do it yourself. If you don't care, go ahead. With a mouthful of barely chewed meat loaf and mashed potatoes, I'll complain to my wife that our kids have absolutely no table manners. Kids look to you on how to act in public. If you say "please" and "thank you" a lot, so will they. If you fart in church and pick your nose in public, they will too.

Probably the easiest way to demonstrate this is with cursing. This is a tough area for people from the punk scene because we've elevated swearing to an art form, using crass expletives when they are totally unnecessary or when we've just completely run out of things to say. Sometimes I'll be on the phone and won't even notice them coming out of my mouth, or that my kids are listening in for future vocabulary reference. It got so bad that a neighbor brought our kid back from a play date saying my darling daughter had asked their child where the "fucking" ball went. I knew it had gone too far when the same daughter was putting her doll to sleep and said, "Night, night, my little fucker." I started watching the words I used so my kid didn't tell her teacher where she could shove her homework assignment, although it would be funny.

Another important principle we've discovered the hard way is putting in the advance work to head off a bad situation. Once my wife and I took the four- and six-year-old to the House of Pancakes for the first time, and on the way I was telling them what a great place IHOP was, and that they could get the Mickey Mouse pancakes with the raisin eyes and the whipped cream smile and the cherry nose and everything. When we were finally seated, the kids were so excited that they were bouncing off the walls, screaming and knocking things over like a couple of raging chimpanzees in heat. After ten minutes of this, the people in the booth next to us got up and moved to another table and our waitress gave us a dirty look and everyone in the entire restaurant started to stare at Jennifer and me and shake their heads. I scooped both the girls up, took them out into the parking lot, and started yelling at them for making us look bad. I threatened to confiscate their Barbie dolls and keep them as hostages until they learned how to behave and spouted other forms of mental child abuse and basically became psycho dad in the parking lot until they finally settled down and agreed to act civilized. By this point, however, our trip to IHOP had been ruined, and we went home. I didn't realize until I was driving away that it was completely my fault.

I had been so busy building up the trip to the pancake house and telling them how much fun it was going to be that I forgot to do the advance work and set boundaries and consequences before we entered the premises. I should have explained to them that there are still certain rules of behavior in restaurants that don't have giant cheesy rats as mascots, and that they would have to remember their manners and respect the other customers by keeping their voices down if they wanted to sample the culinary delights of a sophisticated place like IHOP. If I had prepared them in advance I wouldn't have needed to go postal in the parking lot and missed out on a blueberry short stack myself. If I'd set the limits beforehand, we would have had a great time and they would have respected my authority, but instead I told them what a great time they were going to have, then yelled at them when they tried to. I suck!

In almost every situation where our kids misbehave, I can probably think back and realize that if I would have just given them some advice on how to act beforehand, we could have avoided a bad situation. Now I try to tell them how they'll be expected to behave in a given situation in advance so I don't have to blame myself when they act like most kids do, which is totally unhinged and out of control. If you give them a little heads up on what will be expected of them when they go to school, or out to dinner, or on a play date, it might help avoid a lot of the trouble they will ingeniously and spontaneously think of getting into, and you won't have to think up creative new ways to punish them for it.

To some extent I've tried to make it seem like I'm on my kids' side and that the consequences of their bad behavior will result in me having to play the tough dad role and dole out punishment should they choose to continue down the path they're on when they're acting up. Some parenting wizard will probably be able to find a problem with this approach, but for now, it works for me. For example, I'll say, "If I was you, I'd be on your best behavior tonight out at dinner and not fight with each other, because if you use your manners and act nice, we might be able to stop and get some ice cream afterward. If you don't, we'll have to leave and you won't get anything." This way I'm coaching them on how to do the right thing so this third person—"authoritative dad"—won't have to come out. I'm looking out for their best interests, and, of course, my own. Having a peaceful dinner is better than the alternative and the ice cream afterward was my idea in the first place.

Some experts criticize the reward-for-good-behavior technique, but what do they know? Experts are experts at having theories no one can prove. I think rewarding good behavior sets them up for a time in their life when they'll have to show up at work every day and act civil and work hard to get their paycheck, and if they act lazy and disobedient they'll get fired. There's not a much better life lesson than that. Obviously, you don't want to get to a point where you're training your kid like a circus seal, holding sardines over their head to get them to do what you want, but by letting them know that if they resist the impulse to act like a little spaz and can control their behavior in certain situations they might get compensated in some way, they'll have more incentive to do so. Conversely, if they know there could be a sharp penalty for misbehavior, they'll probably be less inclined to engage in the types of activities that give me a major headache.

TIME-OUTS

Even with positive discipline and rewards and praise for the times when they don't freak out and embarrass you at a restaurant, sometimes the temptation to misbehave is too great for some kids. Who am I kidding? Sometimes it's too much for forty-year-old dads as well. Although it sounds easier than it is, the only acceptable means of disciplining your kids these days is by giving a "time-out" or by taking away privileges. I know in the old days our dads just used their belts on us, but nowadays the lightest spanking could get you sent up the river on child abuse charges.

Time-outs involve taking your kid to a prearranged spot for a prearranged amount of time to let them chill out and collect themselves when they're behaving in a way that's unacceptable. This spot shouldn't be their bedroom because being sent to the place where they keep all their toys isn't much punishment. Once the time-out is over we have a brief conversation with them and explain why they were given the time-out, what type of behavior we expect of them and what behavior will get them put right back sitting next to the cat box. Taking away privileges obviously means not letting them do something they enjoy doing, like watching TV, riding their bike, or chewing gum, anything they get enjoyment out of and will be bummed out that they won't get to do. It won't help if the privilege you take away is something vague or indeterminate, like threatening to take away their right to vote or use the bathroom. It has to be something they will sorely miss, like a video game or their favorite shoes.

We've also found that it's incredibly important to be consistent and present a united front. If we threaten a time-out or a taking away of privileges but then one of us fails to follow through, our kids will only try to get away with it that much harder the next time. It has to be a foregone conclusion in their mind and ours that the prewarned discipline for misbehavior will be carried out no matter how many tears, curses, and boo-boo lips it causes or it loses all its power. If we're not consistent and follow through when we threaten to take away Christmas, they think they can get away with anything.

FREEDOM OF CHOICE

When it comes to getting them to do things they don't want to do, one thing that I've found works sometimes is giving them a choice so they can decide between two things you want them to do instead of just refusing to do anything. My two-year-old has a thing about shoes. She will only wear the ones she is in the mood for at a particular time and they're usually the ones that are completely inappropriate for what she's wearing on the rest of her body—the black shiny tap shoes with her pajamas or snow boots with her sundress—but most of the time she doesn't want to wear any shoes at all. She can sense the times when we're going to a nice place for dinner to choose when she wants to go barefoot, then starts to freak when I demand she wear something on her feet. Before she goes completely postal, I take her to the closet and give her a choice of which shoes to wear. "I like the pink Vans slip-ons with tiny skulls on them, but Mom likes the pink Doc Martens. Which ones do you want to wear?" Now that she has a little control over the situation she's more likely to capitulate. Either that or she'll refuse and I'll have to get into a no-holds-barred wrestling match with a two-year-old as I try to strap her feet into a pair of sandals. One way or another she'll be leaving the house with shoes on, I tell myself. It's really degrading when I come to the car with a barefoot child who's smiling like Alexander the Great after a fierce battle victory.

CHOOSING YOUR BATTLES

Here's a scenario. You wake up in the morning and the kid won't get dressed so you say, "Well then, we can't go to the park," and they freak out. You give them a choice of what to wear, and after a little while of moping around and kicking furniture, they let you dress them, and you go. When you get home they want to watch television, but you say, 'no,' they watched enough this morning, and they flop on the floor and start crying and kicking until something else gets their attention and they go play with that. Later on, you're at the grocery store and they scream for a candy bar, but you say no because it will spoil their dinner. They have a total freak-out attack and you ignore them and leave the area. After dinner that night you say they can't leave the table until they eat their peas, they refuse and sit there staring at the offending peas for close to an hour. After they eat them they ask if they can have a scoop of ice cream and watch a video, you say yes because you've said no so many times today, and they deserve a break, and you really don't want another meltdown while you're reading an old issue of *Flipside*. Then you tell them to brush their teeth, put on their pajamas, and go to bed and they have another total meltdown. Overall, you score the day 5–1, advantage: parents, not too bad.

The point of this is something called "Choosing Your Battles." Kids are going to have freak-outs and temper tantrums all day in an effort to get what they want. If you give in every time, you're screwed. The kid will run you and the household and you won't have a life. If you're too harsh and never let them have any fun they'll eventually hate you and could come after you with a blunt object one day. Picking your battles lets you say no when you really need to for your best interests and theirs, and it establishes that you are in control in the relationship, but then letting them have a break every once in a while, like sharing a bag of peanut M&Ms with them, lets them know you can be cool sometimes as well.

Although I can pontificate on how consistency and presenting a united front is key in every situation, there have been times when we've been so inconsistent with our kids they probably wonder what parent is going to show up on a given day. Sometimes we are on top of our game, correcting the misbehavior, leading by example, and doling out fair, consistent punishments, but other times we're so beat we just give up and let them do whatever the hell they want. This is why sometimes they behave like perfect angels, while others, they are totally out of control. They're completely caught off guard when they start misbehaving and the disciplinarian parents show up and they get grounded for a week.

Some kids are just incredible challenges and no matter what you do, it's just not going to be easy; in fact, raising them will probably include some type of prescription medication for you and eventual hard time in juvenile hall for them, while other kids will be a breeze. The truth is there's only so much we can do. Do too much and you'll have an extremely well-behaved robot kid who hates your guts; do too little and you'll have a miniature Napoleon bully who won't be prepared to accept responsibility for anything they do later in life. If I've done my part to try to be a good parent but they still steal the neighbor's car and flip off the principal at school, there comes a point where you just have to throw up your arms and say, "Well, I did my best. It's society's problem now."

ANARCHY IN THE PRE-K

One of my official duties as punk rock dad when I'm not cruising the aisles of record stores looking for rare copies of Stiff Little Fingers albums is that of family videographer. I have to make sure I capture every birthday blowing out of candles, every flour-covered face helping cook pumpkin pie on Thanksgiving, every shining new bicycle or Barbie fun house being unwrapped on Christmas morning, and every multicolored egg being discovered hidden behind a tree on Easter, all in vivid digital detail. There has been weeping, cursing, and great gnashing of teeth for the multiple times I accidentally left the cap on the lens or ran out of tape or battery life and failed to document one of our cherished family memories on Super 8 video. My penance now is to be asked repeatedly before each new event if the lens cap is off, if the battery is charged, and if there is enough tape in the camera to capture each and every newly toothless smile and hopeful birthday wish for posterity.

Pre-K is the modern term for preschool and these days if your kid isn't enrolled in one as soon as they can walk and talk, neighborhood watch monitors will accuse you of reckless child endangerment. My children were, of course, first in line, as my wife, like all the other mommies in the newly yuppified South Bay, intends for her children to have every advantage in life when it comes to education. While I think they'd do well to be allowed to play around a little unsupervised before they have to face fifteen straight years of teachers, detention, and backpacks filled with a hundred pounds of homework, I reserve judgment and agree to serve my role as occasional picker upper or dropper offer of our toddler and full-time video documentarian.

The last school function I was in charge of filming was the Halloween parade. I'd brought my trusty camcorder, checked the lens, battery, and tape, and stood outside the classroom with a couple of other equally disheveled-looking dads who either didn't have a day job, were independently wealthy, or sold drugs while their wives made millions in real estate. Just inside the door to one of the classrooms, Batman was leaning out the door crying and looking for his mommy until a teacher dressed up like a Krispy Kreme donut came over and consoled him. Soon a bell rang and the playground in front of us was instantly covered by dozens of small costumed creatures who came pouring out of the classrooms and were bumping into each other because many of them couldn't see through their sweaty plastic masks. For a moment there, the swirling spectacle of all the vivid colors, garish costumes, and general pandemonium threatened to give me a bad acid trip flashback. There were small, frilly Cinderellas,

Snow Whites, and Sleeping Beauties wearing lighted tennis shoes, miniature boxy Sponge Bobs, and Ariel mermaids in outfits that seemed impossible to walk or sit down in, as well as diminutive Buzz Lightyears and brawny Supermen, various Draculas, army guys, assorted monsters wearing masks with eyeballs hanging down their face, and plenty of Teenage Mutant Ninja Turtles, even though this particular show had fallen out of favor among most kids years ago.

At one point someone blew a whistle and everyone was told to line up by class and soon all the three-foot creatures were bumping into one another and jostling for position in line and this was when my little fairy princess usually runs into problems. Daughter number two always has to be first, in everything. First to walk out the door, first into the car, first to use the bathroom, first in the snack line, first to do just about anything, but definitely first in line. She will bump, cross check, and body block anyone she has to if the position is open, and has been known to take out many children twice her size to gain her rightful spot at the head of the line. Although anticipating the whistle, she assumed her rightful position unchallenged, a Buzz Lightyear took exception when his spot just behind her was cut in front of by a Mutant Ninja Turtle and a small skirmish broke out. Unfortunately for little Buzz, the death ray laser beam he fired from his cuff link was little more than a battery-powered tiny red light-bulb, and before the teacher dressed as the wicked witch could intervene, the mutant turtle sent him to the blacktop with a fairly professionally delivered mutant ninja turtle spinning back kick. For some reason I watched the spectacle transfixed instead of filming it and lost out on an assured ten thousand dollar prize on *America's Funniest Home Videos*.

Preschool class consists of a lot of storytelling, finger painting, marching in line to and from different places, and playing on the playground. It's basically just school without much schoolwork. They learn about saying the Pledge of Allegiance (I tell my kids to defiantly raise a single fist in protest during the "Under God" part just to piss off the conservative parents in class) and also about how to sit still on a rug and listen to the teacher and not just run around the room the whole time like a crazy person. Without this small bit of practice, they can hardly be expected to know how to behave in kindergarten if they've been sitting home watching *Sesame Street* all day, although they'll probably know the alphabet really well.

Every time one of our children started kindergarten there's always one or two kids there who are scared to death, crying and freaking out because it was their first experience with being dropped off to hang out with a bunch of other kids all day with no mommy around to hold their hand. Daughter number one, being the sketchy child, wasn't particularly thrilled about it, either, her first day, but after having spent two full years in preschool she knew what to expect somewhat and was able to handle it with only a few scenes of clinging to her mom's leg.

I thought wild-woman daughter number two would bring home so many yellow and red cards from climbing walls and putting other kids in headlocks that I would have a full deck by the first month, but amazingly she instead brought home a few gold cards for good citizenship. Somehow a great preschool teacher and some quiet time on the carpet tamed the savage beast within her and taught her that she needed to maintain control in the classroom and save the spazzing out for the monkey bars during recess.

Daughter number two may be a little hellion at home because she feels comfortable enough to cut loose, but at school she feels the pressure to excel just like she does in sports. She wants to get good grades and not be embarrassed by being reprimanded in class all the time so she usually tries to be on her best behavior. She knows that it's only at home she can get away with things like calling her dad a "butt munch" or throwing her food across the table.

The great part of this for the punk rock dad was that, when I wasn't on tour, I could be home to drop off or pick up the kids at preschool and have a chance to be involved in their daily lives. There were more than a few times I found myself outside the classroom waiting for the kiddies to be dismissed, standing in a circle of moms trading stories about some funny thing their kids said, or gossiping about what a horrible parent that one mom was in Room Four, and who does she think she is taking up three spaces with her Hummer in an already crowded parking lot and I bet her nanny hates her. Then I snap out of it and think, "What the hell am I doing?" and grab my kid and run.

THE LAND OF COMPETITION

When the kids entered pre-K, I knew that this was the beginning of decades of interaction with other parents in the community, and I wasn't surprised to find out that most of them weren't raised listening to Black Flag and the Adolescents and sneaking into punk shows. Although 95 percent of the parents we deal with on a day-to-day basis are normal, nice, well-adjusted people, because the home prices in Southern California have nearly quadrupled in the last decade, some of the parents we rub elbows with at school functions and little league games are of a completely different social variety than the working families native to the area. The new breed of power parents are entertainment lawyers, dot-com moguls, and security bonds traders with three nannies, four gardeners, two on-call plastic surgeons, and no problem paying cash for a five-million-dollar McMansion overlooking the ocean.

Driving around our little hippie beach community in the 1960s, you would have seen peace-loving surfers with ARMS ARE FOR HUGGING stickers on the backs of their VW vans, with naturally tanned surfer girls riding next to them and dinged-up long boards strapped to the roof. Now you'll find heavily Botoxed and silicon-enhanced soccer moms driving luxury SUVs with GPS satellite systems guiding them to the nearest Starbucks or tanning booth. Dad tools around in the latest Mercedes S-Class "I wish my d@#k was bigger" convertible coupe, and has his own personal trainer to help shape his microliposuctioned, hair-free abs. This is all so they can sleep well at night on their six-thousand thread count sheets, knowing they are not only keeping up with the Joneses, but thanks to their thousand-dollar-a-day personal trainer, they could thoroughly kick the Joneses' asses.

I woke up early one morning last summer and decided to drive down to the beach and check the waves, and listen to an old Naked Raygun cassette tape I'd found that I used to play over and over when I was just out of college. I pulled out of my driveway and was slowly driving down our quiet residential street when I was nearly run off the road by a crazed woman coming around the corner taking her kids to a nearby school in a giant SUV. I swerved out of the way and she blasted her horn at me, yelled some profanities, flipped me off, and disappeared in a cloud of exhaust and large "RE-ELECT BUSH" and "AYSO SOCCER" stickers in her back window.

Many of these nouveau riche supercompetitive parents hyped up on gallons of triple nonfat lattes are completely crazed with the need to prove the genetic superiority of their little slice of heaven's goodness against your evil spawn of Satan, and will treat this competition like a battle of biblical proportions. At our elementary school, and I swear to you this is not a lie, the mom's start to camp out at one o'clock in the morning and spend the entire night shivering in line to get priority to sign their kids up for the best classes and best teachers. What's this about? How can there be a bad teacher in kindergarten? Does one of them put acid in the finger paint? Is there one kindergarten teacher who's out on parole, sitting alone in a classroom with her crayons because no one wants their kid to take her class? Is their some hidden network of mommies that sends e-mails to each other saying, "Don't take Ms. Ryan's class. She's a known cannibal"?

Psycho soccer moms and dads are everywhere. From far away they may look like normal people in their $500 sunglasses and designer stressed jeans, but don't let looks fool you. To them, raising children is the Olympics, the Super Bowl, and the Iditarod, all blended into one huge battle royale. They want their kid to win every event at any cost, and are willing to do almost anything to make sure they get every advantage in life, and trampling over your little youngster along the way may just have to be part of the price. This aberrant behavior comes from our animal instinct to protect and provide for the welfare of our offspring. The desire to perpetuate the survival of our gene pool is hardwired into our DNA, but some modern parents don't realize we're not on the African serengeti anymore, and they no longer have to eat the young of those who challenge their child's position in the pecking order.

The other place the psycho parents show their true colors is on play dates and in social situations at school. They compulsively have to be involved in every small bit of social interaction in their children's lives, suffocating everyone with their extreme butting-in to a point where you'll wonder if they're not out there on the playground throwing elbows for their kid in line for the monkey bars. They'll be best friends with all the teachers and principals and can be seen chatting up the janitors and P.E. coaches between classes, hoping to win some influence for their child. They'll volunteer to be the teacher's assistant's helper's aide, cutting out paper hearts for the Valentine's Day party and posing motionless for thirty-six straight hours in the manger for the Christmas pageant. They'll build a life-size replica of a haunted house for the Halloween carnival, dye seventeen thousand eggs for the Easter parade, and on Martin Luther King Day, they'll mime a dramatic reenactment of the assassination in real time. If need be, they'll drive the school bus on field trips, resod the kickball field, and when there's nothing left to do, they'll just drive around and patrol the perimeter of the campus in their luxury minivans, listening to self-improvement tapes. In their bold, naked attempts to curry the smallest bit of favor for their richly deserving offspring, they'll bring ass kissing and brown nosing to previously unheard of levels. You'll want to puke.

PARENTING GROUPS

So I was pretty concerned with what I was getting into when my wife signed us up for the requisite parenting groups and mommy and me classes. I figured all the other parents would be of the psycho conservative variety and that I'd stand out as the lone punk rock dad in the room and have nothing in common with any of them. I was pissed off at first at having to go to all these get-togethers where you have to socialize with a bunch of people you don't know and eat fancy finger foods and drink cocktails and wine instead of beer. For us dads, at first, much of the time was spent in a semicircle with about six other guys in Tommy Bahama shirts, discussing sports scores and playoff results, and a lot of the time you're kind of shuffling back and forth looking at your shoes not knowing what to talk about and feeling uncomfortable. Then we have a couple more margaritas and everyone begins to loosen up a bit and we start trading stories about things we did in high school and then someone mentions they were at the same Ramones show I was in 1985 and I begin to realize that although some of them may have entered the corporate world and wear the uniform, like me they're all still kids at heart in a grown-up world and like to get into trouble occasionally like we used to, it's just that now the hangovers last a little longer and we all have kids who want to be played with on the weekends. After a while we start taking shots together, and before I know it I'm enjoying myself so much I'm pissed off when Jennifer says we have to leave.

The truth is we've made some lifelong friends in our parenting groups, and to be honest, it's great having friends who aren't from the same walk of life as I am, and who may have differing views from my own pessimistic outlook on life. They all thought it was funny that I was in a punk band and joked that they wanted to quit their jobs and come work as roadies for us. It's great getting together with people who, although they may not have grown up going to punk shows and sporting Mohawks like I did, have the exact same frustrations, concerns, and funny diaper stories as we do, and this commonality we share transcends the barriers of political opinion and taste in music. Hopefully I've opened some of them up to some alternative ways of looking at the world, and they've taught me not to be such a self-righteous asshole.

Although some parents are more open-minded and willing to accept the friendship of the punk rock family, others aren't as accommodating. Unfortunately for her, my somewhat shy conservative wife is usually the one who has to bear the burden of me being in a patently offensive, left-leaning punk band in an area that is becoming more and more of a Republican stronghold. A while back, a new family moved into the neighborhood with a daughter close in age to daughter number one, and they immediately had a few play dates and opened a lemonade stand together. When the other mom inevitably asked what I did for a living, Jennifer gave up the information piecemeal, "He's a musician," "It's a punk band," and when prodded for the band's name, reluctantly added, "It's called Pennywise, but I'm sure you've never heard of it," knowing the information would probably scare her off. The wife, of course, responded that she would look us up on the Internet, and the next day there were no more play dates, the lemonade stand was closed down, and now we only get a forced wave when we drive by their house.

I could act like this attitude is totally reprehensible, but the truth is, if my kid came home and said she wanted to have multiple play dates with a kid whose parents were into some religious cult I didn't agree with, it might be hard for me not to censor who they are allowed to play with. This is unfortunate because without all of their parents' dogma getting in the way, most kids just want to play and sell lemonade together. I've slowly come to find out that instead of reinforcing my initial feeling that punk rock moms and dads would be completely different and stand out from all the rest, most of my interactions with other parents have actually shown me how much we're all the same.

6

WE'RE A HAPPY FAMILY

We were all in the grocery store a while back and the two-year-old was cranky because she didn't get a nap, and the other two didn't want to be there because they wanted to be home watching TV or playing with the kids up the street, but the problem was, we had to eat, so dragging everyone along to make sure we all get what we want seems to be the best way to accomplish this. Daughter number two, who is lactose intolerant, needed Lactaid milk, daughter number one, who won't eat meat, needed beans and cottage cheese and almonds so she could get enough protein to continue to grow, and Jennifer, the near-vegetarian, needed enough vegetables and salad ingredients to feed a large army of rabbits. I needed to go along so I could get the junk food my wife won't buy for me and TV dinners for the nights when, because of our peculiar dietary habits, I need the familiar comfort of a tray of Salisbury steak and mashed potatoes just to feel somewhat normal.

The problem occurred when we took our bulging cart to the checkout stand and the two-year-old saw the gum display near the register and started absolutely freaking out for it. Daughter number three is a complete gum junkie. She needs her fix several times a day, everyday, and comes waddling up to me when I'm on the computer, playing guitar, or watching TV, crying, "Daddy, I need guuuuuuuuummmmm," pulling on my shorts and giving me a mournful look like a desperate addict unable to kick the habit. When I said no she started arching her back and turning red and pulling her hair and making a total spectacle of herself. Now the checker and people in line were giving me dirty looks and shaking their heads like I was the worst parent in history because I couldn't control my kid. I thought to myself that it wasn't my fault that of all the millions of sperm in my sack, only the superspastic one was hyper enough to pierce the egg, but now I just wanted the spectacle to end so I could get my life back and buy my Hungry Man TV dinner in relative peace. So I gave up and handed her the goddamn stick of gum, and then, of course, Jennifer immediately said, "Now she's going to do that every time she wants something." Knowing that spousal abuse would get me five to ten at Folsom, I wanted to crawl into a cooler in the frozen food section and slowly freeze to death.

When I'm not touring, my wife and I get to spend a lot of time together. The most common argument we get into is over what I call "armchair parenting." One of us will observe the other person doing something with the kids and when something goes wrong we point out how we would have handled the situation better. You go on to say how you can't understand how you partner could be so stupid to do it that way, like you're the world's foremost child-rearing expert, when in reality you've probably done much stupider things, like putting the baby's sleeper on upside down.

Everyone knows the officially sanctioned right thing to do in most cases, but a lot of times there are circumstances that make it so that doing the right thing will cause you such emotional trauma and extreme social embarrassment that you may have to ignore a few pages from the parental handbook momentarily just to survive. This is real life, not a parenting book. There are many times when you just plain screw up royally. No one wants to be told in the heat of the moment they're doing a horrible job of parenting. You know this better than anyone and probably don't need to be reminded. I do this every time my wife has trouble negotiating a conflict with the kids, and I should be brought up on charges at the next parenting group meeting for it.

There are times under the stress of parenting that can bring out the best and worst in all of us, and we all have different personalities when it comes to handling it. My particular personality profile seems to feel that blaming my wife when something goes wrong is the most rational thing to do in most situations. My wife has termed this habit "Asshole Behavior," or "Being an Asshole," but I'm working on it. We've found that the best ways to deal with these marital conflicts are short periods of bad vibes and general avoidance therapy. Being the consummate blamer, whenever I'm in another room and hear my child cry out in pain or fright, I come storming in, pick up the poor child, throw my wife an icy stare, and say, "What did you do to her?" Like she was in there pinching her or something. Fingers slammed in the door? Why didn't my wife lock it? Baby falls down and bonks her head? Why wasn't she watching her? Baby catches cold? Why the hell did she take her out of the house in the first place? Luckily, at least I know when I'm being an a-hole, and a few moments later I usually come back and sheepishly apologize, to which my wife responds with a raised middle finger. We're working on our communication skills.

A lot of parents constantly differ on the way kids should be disciplined. If you were brought up in a very strict disciplinarian household where you were spanked and locked up in a cage on the weekends, you're either going to feel your kids should be raised the same way or you're going to remember how awful it was and not want to put your kids through the hell you went through. Chances are better it will be a mixture of both. Sometimes you'll want to do it the nice way, but other times, the idea of a nice, comfortable toddler kennel won't seem that irrational.

The new parenting will be hard for some of the more militant dads out there to swallow. These days we don't spank, yell, threaten, ridicule, or criticize. We reason with our children and talk to them like we're the Dalai Lama in a calm, reassuring voice so we don't dent their fragile psyches. This type of discipline doesn't leave a lot of options for guys who were raised knowing that if they socked their sibling in the mouth, or stole money from their mom's purse, they'd be spending some quality time with the business end of their dad's leather belt when he got home from work. We knew that particular form of deterrent worked perfectly well when we were young, and not having it as a last resort when your kid sorely deserves it leaves us feeling a little de-fanged in the discipline area. Although, for the most part, my wife and I agree on the acceptable means of disciplining our children, I still complain that I'm not allowed to use the one foolproof method when none of them work.

Parenthood isn't solely about your kids. As they get older, we have to work even harder at getting along with our partner by communicating and presenting a united front and all that other garbage, when, in reality, it seems like we disagree on every detail of how our future Mozarts should be raised. There are a plethora of parental conflicts to be negotiated here, not the least of which is the issue of resentment that the wife can form when she's left home taking care of the kids while dad is out working at some job where he gets to take three-hour martini lunches and go golfing with the boss on the weekends, just because he's the breadwinner. For me, it's when I go on tour and she's home breaking up fights and trying to put three kids to bed and cleaning up after them all day, while I'm on a tour, drinking beer and playing video games on a tour bus, that things begin to seem a little one-sided. When dads get home and are ready to relax after a hard day of work, their wives are expecting them to step up and do their share of parenting and crowd control, which they've been covering single-handedly when the dads were not around. This is the eternal conflict of parenting that, without good communication and an active sex life, can easily lead to bad vibes, shouting matches, and divorce court.

SHARING HOUSEHOLD DUTIES

The sharing of household and family duties is an issue that can create a lot of tension and conflict, but we've found that with a little advance work it can sometimes be handled with a modicum of civility instead of open hostility. Some jobs traditionally fall along gender lines if everyone is okay with it. I take out the trash and do most of the heavy lifting and jobs that require scaling ladders, unclogging toilets, killing spiders, and doing gross things, while she usually handles the cooking and laundry and dressing of Barbies and braiding of hair and things that require smaller hands and a more feminine touch. Some may see these gender-based delineations as being sexist, but if a couple is more gender confused, where, for example, the guy likes to drink wine, listen to the Smiths, and read French poetry, while she chugs 40s, cranks up the G.B.H., and starts her own one-woman mosh pit in the living room, I'm sure it's okay to reverse the assignments.

There are a couple of trade-offs with household duties that seem to work well for us. One is that at dinnertime, whoever cooks, the other cleans. I rarely cook so that means I spend a lot of time with my hands in the suds or loading and unloading the dishwasher. That's fine with me because it's a great time to practice my transcendental meditation, unless we had something for dinner that stuck melted cheese on the plates or greasy sludge to the sides of the pots and pans because then I tend to forget all about the Buddhist nonsense and lose my shit completely. I think my wife knows she has it easy because who doesn't like to cook? It's basically just experimenting with food and making a huge mess for someone else to clean up and pretending you're on one of those cooking shows "reducing" and "sautéing" instead of just cooking things. Afterward it's my job to try to put the kitchen back together. I think everyone prefers this because they've all had my version of meat loaf, where it looks more like a burnt meat cracker and tastes like an old mattress, so no one's complaining about the arrangement.

COMMUNICATION BREAKDOWN

When a guy is just sitting around not saying anything, most women will have to ask them what they are thinking about. You should never tell them the truth: that your mind is a swirl of pornography, sports scores, food, and a constant running down of a list of people you'd like to punch in the mouth. They want you to say that you're thinking about her and how wonderful she is, and that you were trying to come up with ways to make your relationship more romantic, and just wishing you two had more time to talk and cuddle.

My wife has to tell me things a hundred times because she knows I'm usually not listening. Sometimes it seems that what she's saying is just an endless list of things she needs me to remember to do and eventually my mind just shuts down and doesn't hear her anymore. I don't think I've ever gone to the store and made it back with everything she asked for. I always end up taking two trips. She starts running down her list for me as I'm walking out the door, and about halfway through, after broccoli, diapers, and toilet paper, my brain goes on autopilot. It's gotten to the point now where she has to say, "Look at me when I'm talking to you," like I'm a child, but I can't really blame her.

There's a difference between talking, communicating, and discussing. I love talking with my wife. We're best friends and talk to each other all the time. "Talking" consists of agreeing with each other what a bunch of complete psychopaths all our friends and family members are, and bantering about what we're going to have for dinner, and includes all the pleasant conversations we have where no one goes away angry. "Communicating" is done when one of us has a problem or issue and needs the other person to agree with whatever we are saying. If the conflict isn't resolved when we are "communicating," this can lead to a "major discussion," which is basically how most people communicate just before couple's therapy.

When Jennifer comes to me with a problem, my natural instinct is to want to solve it. She complains that there's too much laundry around the house, so I offer to buy her a bigger washer or build more shelves in the closet. One of the moms at school is a total psycho? I offer to have the person "rubbed out." Everything she complains about I want to take to Home Depot and find a quick-fix repair kit for it so I don't have to hear about it. The real problem is that most women just want to have someone to listen to and commiserate with all the frustrations they have to deal with every day, and be sympathetic to what they're going through. It probably does suck dealing with the pressures she's put under, just like it does for me, and sometimes just having your soul mate listen and encourage you might be all you need to get through it. I tell my wife all the time that I couldn't have picked three bigger morons to share a band with if I lived under a moron band member tree, and she just listens and probably thinks they have the exact same problem. The best part is, she listens to me, or at least I think she does. I tend to bitch a lot.

THE SOPHOMORE SLUMP

At one point after our second daughter arrived, I realized that I was staying home being the dutiful dad all the time, while my friends were going out every night and seeing shows like I used to before we had kids. Feeling envious and thinking my life was passing me by and that I was missing out on all the fun, I started to go out with the boys a few weekends in a row, coming home drunk and obnoxious at 3 A.M. and being hung over the entire next day. Jennifer wasn't too impressed with this behavior and let me know about it. Of course I got resentful and told her she was just trying to bring me down and turn me into a eunuch like my friends said she was.

After years of being a great dad and being responsible, a lot of dads feel they deserve a reward and sometimes end up rewarding themselves for a decade or more. There's no doubt that one thing that has suffered since I've become a dad has been my social life, although if I was so concerned with that, I would never have agreed to have kids in the first place. The great thing about your friends is that they'll always be there for you to call up the next day and tell you what a great party you missed last night, and how they had the best time ever, and you blew it by not going, and hope you had fun staying home and watching TV with the kids and changing diapers all night.

There are plenty of other areas for turmoil when you have kids, but with some forethought, you can avoid all the stupid arguments that end up splitting some families apart, families that with a little bit of structure might have pulled it off. The problem lies with learning to argue fairly, if such a thing exists. In parenting books they always say, criticize the behavior, not the child. We parents should do the same. Look, if I forget to bring the stroller to the walk in the park, or the snow jacket on the snow-boarding trip, or the sippy cup on the three hour drive, let's plan to make a checklist next time, instead of calling me "Rain Man," or "Shit for Brains." This doesn't set the best example for the kids. I will then promise not to whisper to the children that Mommy's an escaped mental patient when she somehow finds a way to burn three bowls of oatmeal in a row. None of these negative responses are conducive to effective role modeling. When someone in an argument responds with an insult about some-one's personal appearance or character, it's called an "ad-homi-nem retort," and it's not really fair, and frankly, I'm getting tired of the times when I have a complaint about my wife's house-cleaning skills that I'm told that my "feet stink," or that my "ass smells." Reducing the amount of these hurtful remarks goes a long way in keeping the marriage harmonious.

THE WORLD'S A MESS, IT'S IN MY KISS

I'll be watching the news late at night, observing humanity's continued slide into a living hell of world war, reality TV, and global warming, and then a commercial will come on featuring some bikini-clad model writhing around on a sports car or walking along a sunny beach, and I'll think to myself, "It's been several weeks since we've had sex." With work, school, soccer, and T-ball games, piano lessons, brownie meetings, and dentist appointments, at the end of a long day and the five-hour drama of putting the kids to bed, many nights we end up falling asleep right after the kids. We'll look at each other and realize we haven't had sex since the last presidency, and my

Johnson is about to detach itself to look for someone who will actually use it.

Kids take a lot of time, attention, and energy. After corralling them all day and keeping them out of trouble, we are usually exhausted. Sometimes after a long day, all we want to do is stare in a comatose-like state at the television, eat a pint of Häagen-Dazs, and go to sleep. Every time we do find a chance to get our game on, we think, "Hey, this is great! Now I remember why I liked this so much! Sex is awesome!" Then there will be another late night of putting the kids to bed, our schedules will be out of sync, and it will seem like we won't have a second to ourselves for another decade.

Like most couples we're sometimes forced to schedule "date nights" so we can reconnect with each other and remind ourselves why we had kids in the first place. We'll go to dinner, see a show, watch a movie, or just get an $8 quadruple espresso at some coffee shop trying to take over the free world. We try not to talk about the kids the whole time and instead gossip about people around town and debate world affairs, and dream about moving to the country someday. Then we go home and make sure the kids are asleep and then make our own home movie by reliving our wedding night with the Barry White CD and the motion lotion. We just try to remember not to accidentally switch labels with the Barney tape and send our kids into therapy.

Many couples fall into the trap where after ten years together everything becomes boring and routine. It sometimes gets hard to remember you're both parents and a couple, and not just two people raising kids together. When we were younger we could just drop everything and get busy anywhere we wanted, but with kids running around, this becomes a lot more complicated. Unfortunately we have a bedroom door that has trouble locking correctly, and on more than one occasion daughter number two has been able to burst through our defenses at the most inopportune moments. This is when I explain that Mommy was choking on a Bagel Bite while on her hands and knees on the bed and Daddy was using a new form of Heimlich maneuver to try and jolt it loose from behind, and we don't have any clothes on because we just got out of the shower and I don't know why Mommy was eating a Bagel Bite in the shower, and *"Get out of here, I said."*

An active sex life helps keep the marriage happy and better prepared to weather the tough spots. That, and it's a lot of fun. It's hard to stay mad at someone who's responsible for getting your rocks off. When you can counter any bad vibes with some mattress aerobics it might make you want to start a few more arguments just so you can enjoy making up.

WE'RE A HAPPY FAMILY

Once our kids reached grade-school age we had a whole new set of problems to deal with. Before, I ruled the household with an iron fist like a third-world dictator, or at least pretended to, but now just like any good rebel faction, they've figured out a million different ways to subvert my authority. Keeping the peace with my wife and between the siblings in the household is now my main goal in life. This can sometimes seem like a futile endeavor because peace and quiet is totally boring for kids. Conflict, rebellion, and general pandemonium are fun and exciting. By the time they hit high school there will be so many built-in challenges facing the success of our family unit, I plan on building a bomb shelter in the backyard and not coming out until after graduation.

Up to this point, Jennifer and I have been the main influences in their lives, but now they have their own group of friends telling them what's cool and what's not, and chances are, we as parents will soon be firmly placed on the "not cool" side. It's not that they don't love us anymore, it's just that they begin to exist in their own little world a lot of the time, and being several decades older than them, we could never relate, regardless of how hard I've been trying to hang on to my youth by dyeing my hair and wearing Clash T-shirts. (See book cover.)

When I think back to the days of my youth spent cruising the alleys, beaches, and dirt lots of Hermosa with my friends, I remember how every day seemed like an adventure that lasted a lifetime. Between surfing and skating and going back and forth from the beach to Mi-T Mart for candy and Slurpees, there was a seemingly endless amount of fun to be had. There were all kinds of drama and conflict at school with teachers and principals, the rivalries and popularity contests between friends and classmates, and, of course, the first stirrings of attraction to the opposite sex. Most of our time was spent engaged in some type of activity meant to produce cheap thrills. As a parent, though, you're on a completely different wavelength than you were as a young punk. Now cheap thrills for us are getting a free cable hookup or when you get a hold of the Victoria's Secret catalog before your wife does.

It's not fun to always be the one person constantly grounding your kids and reprimanding them and stifling their good times. Eventually, no matter what I do, I imagine the girls will come to resent me for it unless I just let them do whatever they want and learn their lessons the hard way. We all know how young people get along with figures of authority; even some forty-year-old guitar players still have a big problem with it. The challenge will be how we can help keep them out of too much trouble and keep the peace in our families, so maybe they won't hate me— at least until they turn sixteen.

WHEN THE KIDS ARE UNITED

My sister and I rarely got along growing up. My mom says when they brought me home from the hospital she reached in my crib and yanked out a fistful of hair off my head. Later on, with my surgically repaired crossed eyes still not working correctly, my self-esteem was already low enough, but like any good sister she did all she could to destroy what little bit I had left. The periods of acne and braces during my stomach-churning teen years were met with joyful celebrations, giving her occasion to coin new terms for my appearance, like "Braille face" and "tin grin," and to spontaneously contribute ego-boosting comments like "Your zits kind of divert the attention away from your ugly face." To this day, she still calls me "Goober," lovingly recalling the dorkiest moron to ever grace the television screen on Mayberry RFD.

I think biology has a lot to do with the way siblings relate to each other. There must be unintelligible chemicals in the air between you that dictate whether or not you're socially compatible with certain brothers or sisters or whether you're likely to pummel them. Within a given family you can have two that get along great but another two that would just as soon drown the other in the bath tub than settle down to a nice game of Chutes and Ladders. Some are supportive and friendly with each other and can share toys and play make-believe games and spend hours hanging out peacefully as if they're co-conspirators in some grand sublime play; others, you can tell that if they could get away with it would nudge their little brother into the shark tank at Sea World just to be the only child again. It seems that it's the ones who are barely a year apart like my sister and I who have the most problems. She was a year old and had all the doting attention of my parents focused on her, their little angel in her pink nightgown. Then along comes this little cross-eyed doofus who's always needing his diapers changed and crying to be fed and who's constantly taking all the attention away from their little perfect princess. I might have yanked some hair out of my head too.

Daughters number one and two were born exactly two years apart and go through stages where they fight over everything: toys, the computer, TV shows, who dances and sings better, and who Mom and Dad loves more. They spend the entire day trying to get on each other's nerves. There can be rare periods of time when they seem to get along perfectly, although these relatively tranquil episodes seem to always coincide with times when they want something from us, like a trip to Disneyland or to stay up late to watch *America's Funniest Home Videos* of dads getting hit in the nuts by errant golf balls. They can usually turn it off and on whenever they want, which sometimes leads me to believe their quibbling is done out of sheer boredom. Either way, there are times when we let them work it out for themselves and others when we have to intervene and referee before it goes so far that someone becomes scarred emotionally, or worse, scarred on the side of their head.

Advance work once again is always the key. As much as we could, we tried to impress upon our older kids that the new addition wasn't going to move into their room, take their favorite toys, and replace them, and that we were all part of a family. We tried to make them learn some responsibility for their younger siblings by letting them help take care of them and give them a bath or read them a bedtime story every once in a while. Sometimes this backfired though, like when, as a six-year-old, the barf-phobic daughter pushed her infant sister off her lap and onto the floor when she spit up a little. Offering a lot of praise for older kids when they help out with their younger siblings makes them feel proud and important, and probably less inclined to find ways to want to sell them off into slavery.

Because most kids crave attention and approval, we try and make sure that each kid gets special one-on-one time with each of us so they don't always have to battle for the attention of Mom or Dad. My middle daughter is so starved for it she'll grab a pen and draw a line on a scrap of paper and say, "Daddy, look what I did." If they constantly have to jostle with a sibling, eventually they start to resent the other person and might start beating on them with a salad spoon. We try to avoid the constant bitterness by scheduling time where we can concentrate on each child individually. I usually do this by putting one in the car and going down to check out the waves and then asking them what they want to do, which is usually followed by them wanting to go get a donut. It's not what you do that counts, it's that you do something that gets you to focus on one child at a time, and can possibly get you a maple bar out of the deal.

Experts say you should try to let them settle disputes on their own so they can learn valuable conflict resolution skills they can use later in life. That would be great except whenever we let our kids work things out for themselves, the skill they usually seem to develop is how to rip a toy out of their sibling's hands and then the other learns how to tell on her for it. Teaching them to look for ways to share or find a compromise for whatever they are fighting over is supposed to help them learn to get along, but they usually just get resentful that they had to give up something they wanted. I think the only way you can encourage fair play that they both can live with is by having a set solution or mediation for each type of conflict in advance. Sometimes we'll use a cooking timer to let each person have a set amount of time playing a certain computer game or listening to the CD player, this way at least they only have to fight over who gets to use it first. Eventually the one who ends up having to go second says, "I didn't want to play that game anyway" and then wanders off to play something else and the problem is solved.

At times our siblings can be our best friends in life, and at others, our worst enemies. They can either make us feel like a cherished member of the family, or they can be the ones whose insults cut the deepest, always knowing exactly which buttons to press. Good communication, making sure they don't always have to compete for Mom and Dad's affection, and then having preset methods to resolve the conflicts that will inevitably occur are probably the only things that will keep the ones who don't get along that well from constantly wanting to tear each other limb from limb. In the end, nothing may work, and forty years later you'll still be having screaming matches over Thanksgiving dinner like my sister and me, and continually brushing up on your conflict resolution skills.

I'M SO BORED WITH THE USA

Boredom is a plague for six- through ten-year-olds. My middle cretin is constantly telling us how incredibly bored she is. "This is the boring-est day ever," she'll say, dribbling a couch pillow like a soccer ball across the wood floor of the living room. You can remind them there are starving kids in China who wish they had the luxury of being bored, but this won't lift the heavy lead veil of boring boredom that shrouds their extremely boring everyday lives. Daughter number two needs constant stimulation, be it through playing catch in the backyard, swinging dangerously high on the swings, climbing a tree, skating, biking, spelunking, hang-gliding, fire-walking, basically anything that will keep all of her constantly moving limbs occupied. If she is not sleeping she needs to be climbing, kicking, or punching on something, and her only down time is spent snacking to fuel her never-ending energy supply.

The older one can sit in the corner and quietly read a book for an entire afternoon. At age eight, she read the seven-hundred-and-fifty page fifth installment of Harry Potter in a single rainy weekend. Daughter number one definitely takes after my temperament, so I constantly feel guilty that I'm never doing enough to keep daughter number two happy by running her around the backyard like an underweight border collie. After she has kept a consistent pitched whine of "Dad, will you play soccer with me? Daaaaaad, will you ride skateboards with me? Daaaaaaaaaaaaaaaaaad, will you run a triathlon or build a life-size replica of Stonehenge with me?" I finally drag my lazy ass onto the threadbare lawn of the backyard and engage in an embarrassingly competitive series of games with her where I pretend that I'm not really trying, just in case the neighbors look over the wall and see that my six-year-old is thoroughly kicking my ass in soccer-basketball.

It's easy to be caught up in the trap of training yourself to think you have to constantly entertain your kid. With the best intentions at heart, I saw one neighborhood dad build a two-story high exact replica of an eighteenth-century pirate ship in his front yard at his kid's request. Me and the other dads in the neighborhood would walk by, thinking, "Poor guy, his kid must have a whine like a glass cutter or a dog whistle. She really broke him this time." There was a picture in the paper of him standing next to the hulking mass looking disheveled, with the accompanying article explaining that it took months to build and how much all the materials cost. The headline should have read A BORED KID'S DAD'S CRY FOR HELP.

The solution I've come up with for the "her-being-bored-me-being-lazy" conflict is a trade-off peace treaty agreement, and so far it's worked okay until she figures a way around it. I tell her that at some point every day I will make time to play with her in some way or another, whether it's a game of full-contact Candyland or a Greco-Roman Olympic decathlon of sorts in the backyard for a period of thirty minutes, and in return, she's not allowed to complain that she is bored within earshot of me the rest of the day and drive me crazy.

The payout in this exchange is that I get some relative peace and quiet or at least a few less moments of sheer pandemonium around the house, and to be honest, once we get playing, I love the quality time playing with the little psycho. There's nothing like watching the pure unbridled fun of a kid with her tongue hanging out the side of her mouth, charging at me with the soccer ball, hoping to score between me, the planter, and the swing set, and then the complete and total exhilaration on her face when she does so easily. There's going to be a time coming soon where I will be the lamest, most embarrassing fart bag she's ever known, and she'll run screaming into her room saying she hates me when I refuse to let her go on a cross-country motorcycle trip with a guy she just met at the mall, so dragging my ass into the backyard to be her hero for a little while shouldn't really be that hard to do.

For daughter number two the saving grace is when soccer season comes around. This is the most popular sport on the planet, with thousands of crazed fans going absolutely berserk during the World Cup, but in America, both parents and kids seem to lose interest in it as a national pastime after about the age of nine for some reason. Until your kids reach that age, though, many of your weekends will be spent in a lawn chair on the sidelines next to a cooler on a field of damp grass, watching as small children in brightly colored uniforms, playing for teams with names like the Orange Blossoms and Mighty Green Geckos, chase a ball around for an hour and a half.

The first year she played was great because this is when the kids had little concept for following the rules of the game or strategy and instead just careened around the field in one giant pack, all kicking legs and tangled limbs, a screaming, laughing scrum of childhood humanity. They flailed and bashed away until one of them finally made contact with something besides the air or an opponent's shin and then the ball popped out, and they all screamed and chased it around the field some more. On rare occasions the ball accidentally made it into the net for a goal so we can have something to cheer about, but most of the time we just sat there laughing at the spectacle of it.

That was until daughter number two, the kinetically hyper, athletic, "victory or death" daughter took to the field. The first few games, as soon as the whistle blew, she just joined the traveling pack, kicking away at the ball like everyone else, but during the middle of game three, it was like a lightbulb went off or a switch was flipped inside her head. She ran into the pack, body checked three girls to the ground, arm barred about four of the others out of the way, took the ball, dribbled it the length of the field in a dramatic breakaway, and then booted the ball so hard into the back of the goal it nearly ripped through the netting. She then did this exact same thing six more times during the game.

The rest of the season pretty much continued on in similar fashion, with her asking me after every game, "How many goals did I make today, Daddy?"

"I think seven, but I lost count after you knocked the goal post over that one time."

By the sixth or seventh game, during team huddles, the coach will tell the other players to do whatever they could to help her get the ball. Eventually I had to tell her to ease up because I think some of the other parents were starting to get a little bummed out that their kids had to just sit and watch her score goals most of the game. I thought some of them might ask me for their registration fees back.

We had one of her games at my old junior high school in Hermosa Valley, and while she racked up goals, I looked around and thought about all the memories I'd made there. In sixth grade, on this field, I had made my first lifelong friends, and had kissed a girl for the first time. After that first year of junior high, though, things began to change. Everyone started to brag about how far they went with their girlfriends that weekend, first base, second base, etc. Then we started stealing booze from our parents' liquor cabinets, and my one friend who had older brothers turned us on to smoking after class one day. After that, our grade school innocence was lost forever. As I looked at all the little kids running around the soccer field, with my daughter scoring goals and playing and laughing, I hoped she wouldn't grow up too fast, that she'd hold on to that innocence a little longer than I did, and that for her, sixth grade would seem to last a lifetime.

I LIKE FOOD, FOOD TASTES GOOD!

An Australian promoter's assistant in charge of shuttling me to and from the show told me that his five-year-old kid will eat anything: meat, fish, crab, vegetables, liver, and he'll clean his plate every time. On his birthday he told his son that he could go wherever he wanted for his birthday dinner, McDonald's, Pizza Hut, wherever. The kid chose sushi. Can you imagine? A kid who prefers raw fish over a Big Mac? As an American I find that impossible. He once asked his dad while eating a thick lamb chop if lamb was really a sheep like they'd seen in the countryside or in a barn, and his dad told him it was. He thought about it for a second, shrugged, and said, "Poor sheep," and kept on eating. I instantly hated him.

Our evening meals have never been an easy affair. Our kids have a problem sitting in one place for more than five minutes in general, so getting them to use their manners and stay seated while I'm trying to stuff my own face with food can be a difficult task. Daughter number one has reduced her diet to a point where she now only eats plain pasta and broccoli. She had always been kind of squeamish about gross slimy things. A typical girly-girl, she didn't like snails, fish, or slugs, or anything "disgusting." One day her cousin came over and informed her that scrambled eggs came from chicken butts, bacon was made from dead pigs, hot dogs and hamburgers were made from ground-up cow intestines, and when you ate chicken nuggets, they were the dead bodies of real chickens you were eating. This was all my five-year-old needed to begin her boycott of all foods that ever had a face or walked around a barnyard. Soon she stopped eating everything from Domino's Pizza to Quarter Pounders to Taco Bell tacos, all the staples of an American diet. Now our dinnertime rituals, which were once exceedingly happy affairs where we would gorge ourselves on great cuisine like turkey meat loaf and barbecued ribs, have descended into stressful encounters where Jennifer and I try every trick of parental coercion and persuasion to force feed the hunger striker.

The meals start by daughter number one asking what we are having. Invariably she absolutely hates what we've cooked and tells us it's the worst thing ever and why can't she just have a bagel for dinner. We then explain calmly that her body needs certain proteins and nutrients to develop correctly and that if she doesn't get a well-balanced diet she may stop developing altogether and soon only her fingernails and hair will grow and she'll go into high school looking like a tiny hair ball with claws and how would that look for her senior portrait? Then she gets scared that we're serious and starts to whine and then I start to think why can't we just have one meal where everyone eats what's in front of them and we're all happy and all of a sudden I'm Al Bundy all over again.

During the time when we were trying to get her to keep eating meat, thinking it would help her grow up strong and tall, we made the huge mistake of trying to secretly mix in a little ground-up chicken with some noodles and vegetables and covered it with copious amounts of teriyaki sauce to throw her off the scent, but somehow she found us out. The two-year-old must have tipped her off. Now she eyes every piece of food placed in front of her like a diamond cutter examining a precious stone, scouring its surface for any trace of alien food particles we might have secreted into the mix without her knowing. I have to spend hours explaining to her that the little green specks on her noodles are just basil seasoning that makes them taste better and not tiny pieces of shredded cow or lamb. Even if I beg and plead and try to convince her we haven't doctored up her pesto noodles with ground-up veal, she won't believe me.

Daughter number two isn't picky but she can't possibly stay seated in her chair at the dinner table for more than a minute, which makes me miss the days when she was strapped into a high chair. Daughter number three ate anything and everything up until she was about two and a half, when she started systematically eliminating food items from her diet, and now just wants to drink juice boxes all day.

The reality with kids and nutrition and finicky eaters is that they are usually getting the right amount of food for them. My kids take a multivitamin every day, eat a bowl of whole grain cereal or oatmeal for breakfast, scarf down a sandwich and carrots for lunch at school, and then eat as much yogurt and fruit for snacks in between. We try to limit the synthetic snack foods drenched in sugar, hydrogenated oils, and preservatives because there's probably a lot of truth to the assertion that the chemical additives that make us crave these foods are what's clogging our arteries, turning our insides into plastic, and making us into a country of people who can't fit into a single chair at the movie theater. Here and there, though, when time and availability are short, a Chips Ahoy cookie or bag of chips won't kill them, either.

When dinnertime comes around, it's not surprising, then, that they don't want to eat the braised duck with snow peas recipe we wrote down from the cooking show. We try to keep it as simple as possible so they'll actually eat something and stay seated without me having to yell at them to be quiet and eat the entire meal. They'll usually eat tons of rice, cheese quesadillas, and broccoli, and chug down a big glass of milk, all while they're telling you stories from school that day and singing songs they heard on the radio. As long as they eat something and they're not living in a fast food line, I guess I shouldn't complain that they're not eating enough from the carnivore side of the menu, and considering what I've heard about factory meat farming, I'm sure it's probably only a matter of time before I'm eating a nice rare tofu steak right along with them.

KIDS OF THE BLACK HOLE

The punk generation was one of the first to be brought up with a TV constantly on in the background during our daily lives. It was relatively new technology for our parents, but for us, we can all probably pinpoint each period in our history based on what shows we were watching at the time. Age seven: *Casper* and *Scooby Doo*. Age ten: *Six Million Dollar Man* and *Happy Days*.

Sixteen: *Mork & Mindy*. Over the years, though, I've started to distrust my closest friend. I'm never really sure when I'm not being sold something, whether it's a secretly partisan network news show coloring every bit of news with their party's political agenda, or watching some scripted reality show with a plot line devised to hook you in long enough for not-so-subtle product placement in the background. I never thought Casper or Steve Austin was trying to put one over on me.

Our kids have about seven million channels now to choose from and can easily get sucked into a void for an entire afternoon. TV has always had the power to either teach kids something valuable or to screw them up tremendously. Kids are little tabula rasas and they tend to imitate whatever they see on the screen. When my kids were watching cartoons with whiny, mean-spirited, sassy kids in them, they started behaving this way at home. They thought this was how normal kids were supposed to act. That being said, TV isn't all bad. I know from experience that I probably still wouldn't know the alphabet if it weren't for the hour each day before school I spent watching *Sesame Street* and eating a bowl of Cocoa Pebbles.

It's amazing to me how much the television can hypnotize us into thinking a certain way, influence our spending habits, and play on our darkest fears. After watching TV for a few hours I'm convinced that there are armies of silent, moldy, carbon dioxide killers invading my home, that soon we'll all be attacked by Africanized bees, and that I need tons of Tupperware containers to store all my stuff and plastic discs to move my furniture around. TV has a way of distorting the facts and begins to cloud your ability to look at the world objectively until, one day, you're watching the tube and suddenly realize you just bought a twelve-disc set of R&B classics performed by a guy with a bamboo pan flute for five hundred bucks.

Kids will watch TV for hours on end if you don't keep an eye on them, and the stuff they watch today is usually horrible. There are a couple of good shows here and there that are educational, but to me, most sitcoms are filled with a bunch of snobby, shallow teenagers insulting all the geeks and nerds in valley girl accents, perpetuating the idea that this is how kids are supposed to think and communicate. Maybe some of these shows just put a mirror up to our culture, but many of them become a self-fulfilling prophecy of how kids will behave after watching TV characters with the cool clothes and perfect skin on their favorite shows act this way. I get really disappointed when I notice the kids have left the room and I'm the only one watching.

I know a lot of people who have started to say no TV whatsoever. I could see myself getting to that point soon. It's a problem, though, when everyone at school is talking about the new show on Disney Channel and your kid doesn't know what they're talking about and so they think he's a freak. We severely limit the amount of TV they're allowed to watch and sometimes use taking it away as a punishment when we're really desperate to get them to stop doing something. I'm sure the experts will probably say this is totally messing them up, but we use what we got. I think it's probably best to try and strike a balance between the crappy stuff they watch and some good educational programming. Either that or I'll rip the thing out of the wall and tell them to go play a board game instead.

I JUST WANNA HAVE SOMETHING TO DO TONIGHT

Tonight was a show night for punk rock dad. We're playing three nights at the Henry Fonda Theater in Hollywood with No Use for A Name, Suicide Machines, and Love Equals Death, and after that we have fifteen more shows on the West Coast with two days off in between. The sadistic booking agent has routed it so after L.A. we go through Bakersfield, then up to Santa Cruz for two shows, but instead of going a couple of hours farther north to San Francisco, we go all the way back down to San Diego, then over to Vegas, Salt Lake, and Denver, before making it back up to San Francisco. It looks great on paper to him, but I'm the one who gets to pile in crowded passenger vans, get middle seats between two portly businessmen on an over sold shuttle flight, take long cab rides through rush hour traffic with grumpy cab drivers, and basically zigzag around the western U.S. like a spastic child with an Etch-a-Sketch for the next three weeks.

We are a working-class punk band. We don't have our own Lear jet flying us to shows like Led Zeppelin or Aerosmith, and usually fly coach when we can't use our meticulously monitored frequent flyer miles for an upgrade into the rarified air of business class to sit feeling out of place among the commuting CEOs and business executives. When we can, we splurge on a tour bus, only because we've already paid our dues by doing multiple U.S. and European tours with band and crew piled tight into the back of a Dodge passenger van, sleeping butts to nuts like a package of hot dogs. Our backstage show rider doesn't feature chilled bottles of Dom Perignon and bowls of M&Ms with all the green ones taken out. We're lucky to get a case of lite beer and a bag of Doritos.

There's always a certain amount of dread that accompanies the start of a tour for me because unlike other elder statesmen of rock 'n' roll, like Neil Diamond, who barely break a sweat on-stage crooning out mid-tempo soft rock hits with an industrial fan blowing cool mist through his hair while he serenades his adoring, seated audiences, five nights in a row for the next three weeks, I'm going to scream, and bark, and yell until the veins in my neck bulge and look like they're going to pop out and explode at any minute, singing along to songs that register in about the 250 beats per minute range, in other words ridiculously fast, urging on a seething mass of about a thousand amped-up adrenaline junkies, in a hot, sweaty box of a nightclub somewhere in a decrepit strip mall in middle America. Every night I'll come off stage drenched in sweat looking like I've just stepped out of a swimming pool, my whole body will ache from twisting and contorting and stage diving and crowd surfing and getting scratched, pummeled, and stomped, and my heart will feel like it's about to beat out of my chest. Every night I basically just have a complete human physical and psychological freak-out for an hour and then collapse. Knowing this hour awaits me on my day planner every day for the next several weeks kind of gives me a strange but satisfying stomach ache. My body is rebelling against it, but something in my psyche is saying, "Bring it on!"

So when I'm staring down a few weeks worth of shows, I need some quiet time to mentally and physically prepare for the warfare I'm about to go into. I'd usually be busy getting ready packing my bag full of changes of underwear and socks and jock itch powder, but after school today there was a marathon play date, then a brownie meeting, and at the same time daughter number one has a piano lesson while number two has soccer practice at a local elementary school across town. Jenifer takes the piano lesson and I take daughter number two and her baby sister to soccer so she and I can watch ten screaming six-year-old girls run around a field and not listen to a word their coach is saying. While they're practicing I get to chase the two-year-old around the iron play set built in the 1940s and try to stop her from gnawing on the chipping lead paint of the monkey bars and keep her from following too close behind the three-year-old on the slide, who has double barrels of lime green snot pouring out his nose and a cough like a lifetime smoker. If she catches his cold she'll give it to me, I won't be able to sing, but I'll have to play the shows anyway, and everyone will come away saying the singer's losing it and should hang it up.

When the future soccer star, the two-year-old, and I get home, I sit down exhausted at the Herculean effort it takes just to get two kids in and out of a car four times, when Jennifer gives me a lightly delivered, off-hand comment that sends an electric charge down my back.

"Don't forget I have Bunko tonight."

"You're not serious."

"I told you five times this week and you said you'd remember and that you were okay with it. It's written right there on the calendar."

On the calendar hanging on the kitchen wall, every square-inch box representing a single day in time is covered in multicolored ink pen and pencil scribbles and scrawls of "Dentist Appointment, 10:30. Early school pick-up today 1:30. Swim class 2:30. 4:00 piano. 8:00 Emotional Meltdown," until it looks like some kind of Egyptian hieroglyphic diary of a demented nuclear physicist.

"Are you kidding me? How can I read what that thing says? When did you tell me? I don't remember that. I'm playing a show tonight. We're leaving for tour. I have to pack. There's no way!"

"I know I told you that, and you nodded your head and waved me off and said 'fine, whatever.'"

"Honey, you know that's my response to everything you say to me. I can't do this. There's no way!"

Bunko is basically a dice game women like to play that is really just a thinly veiled device the mommies of America have came up with to give themselves a night off twice a month in order to gather in someone's dining room and drink white wine and gossip. Other covert sham events they've come up with include "Book Club," "PTA meetings," and the generic-sounding, all-encompassing "Girls' Night Out," which is impossible for you to deny them if you ever plan on reciprocating with your own "Guys' Night Out." These are little more than an excuse for my wife to get out of the house for a few hours and make me appreciate what it's like for her when I'm on tour. So tonight, on a night when I have to play a show in Hollywood in a few hours, I'll be in charge of procuring dinner and putting the kids to bed by myself. I fear this more than the three-week torture tour following it.

After Jennifer leaves the house with an "I'll be back whenever," I don't have the strength, ability, or skill to actually cook them dinner myself so I order a pizza and we all plop down on the couch to watch Disney Channel. The sad part is when you realize you're watching the Disney Channel and you've seen the episode already several times, but you're still watching it again anyway. The pizza comes but the big girls don't like the way it tastes, because Mom orders it from somewhere else, and now they say they had pizza for lunch at school anyway, so I end up eating an entire large pizza with the two-year-old, adding to the rapidly expanding fleshy tire around my gut. Now I have to get up and make the older two a gourmet meal of hot dogs, cottage cheese, and carrots, which they both eat only a few bites of in front of the TV but still manage to scatter all over the couch, floor, coffee table, and remote control. Once they finish, I clean up the carnage, flip off the TV, and tell them it's time for baths and bed. I might as well have told them I accidentally flushed all their Barbie dolls down the toilet, judging from the multi-syllabic, "Daaaa-AAAAA-aaaadd!" cry-whine response this announcement receives.

Like most people in the world, I used to really like to watch TV after dinner. First the evening news shows so I can be further convinced of the hopeless trajectory of modern society, then some PBS documentary about the dietary habits of Neanderthals or Carl Sagan's insights into the billions and billions of galaxies, and after that maybe a stupid sitcom or lazy basketball game, and if I was really desperate, a how-to-remodel-your-deck or cook-Peking-duck show. There's nothing like sinking in to the couch with a nice beverage for several hours to be entertained by the mindless distraction of television. Whatever was on the tube, from about six o'clock until the time I started nodding off after Letterman, I'd be watching.

Not anymore. Now my evenings are spent corralling my three kids and begging, pleading, and outright threatening them into getting into bed and falling asleep. I don't think in the ten years I've had kids that I've had one night where of their own volition my kids have said with a yawn and a stretch, "Night, Dad, I'm turning in." No, to a young person, going to bed just means the fun of being a kid has to end for the day, and you are the person who's putting a stop to it. They will use any means necessary to put off, postpone, and thwart my attempts to drive them into slumber. My kids have developed masterful skills at this, and although I face the same techniques of persuasion night after night, I still haven't come up with a zone defense or man-on-man approach that makes it so that at eight o'clock I'm kicking back on the couch with a beer and a *South Park* episode. I used to look forward to my evenings, but now I dread them like they'll be spent with a sadistic dentist.

The process starts with their bath, which they insist on taking all together, three in the tub, which inevitably leads to a fight because someone splashes or dunks or kicks the other, and ends with one of them screaming that they have soap in their eyes. I pluck them out and towel them off and one of them will cry because they weren't plucked out and toweled off first. This is always followed by an episode of nude gymnastics up and down the hallway. There must be something about being freshly clean that inspires kids to want to run and sing and do cartwheels buck naked. Next, of course, they're told to quit goofing off and put on their pajamas. I can yell all I want, but somehow they always get sidetracked on the long walk from the bath tub to the drawer where the pajamas are kept and I'll find them reading a book or playing a game with no clothes on somewhere. Then you yell again, and after about half an hour of trying, they've somehow managed to get the pajamas completely on their bodies, a process that should take less than thirty-five seconds.

Now it's brushing their teeth, using the toilet, and climbing into bed time. This should also take under five minutes but somehow they can't find their toothbrushes, which is amazing to me since I can't really understand how a toothbrush leaves the bathroom area, but they seem to do so nightly. I'm starting to think that sometime in the afternoon they go and hide them just to buy themselves some time later. They must also hide dolly and blanky at the same time because when we can't find them, they instantly begin to go into hysterics at the thought that dolly and blanky could have somehow fallen into a bottomless void or wormhole in time somewhere.

I take the two-year-old in first to try getting her to go to bed, but she wants me to find dolly's "ba-ba" for her, which has been missing for a good six months, but all of a sudden she has to have it *now* and is whining and crying for it. So I tear apart the closets and toy chests until I finally find the right small pink plastic dolly bottle and as soon as she crams it in dolly's mouth, now she doesn't like the outfit dolly has on and wants "the udder one, the udder one!" Which "udder one" I don't know, but she's getting more and more frustrated because she didn't get a nap today and she's getting fussy and mad and crying since I can't find the right outfit. She keeps freaking out until I scoop her up on my back and pretend to be a pony and crawl around on my hands and knees for what seems like hours because if I stop she'll just cry "more, more" and so I just keep going around in circles and neighing and whinnying like a horse and eventually I coax her off with a sippy cup of milk and a promise that I will tell her all three of her favorite bedtime stories, Cinderella, Goldilocks and the Three Bears, and The Three Little Pigs. All of these stories I've forgotten most of the details to so I just make it up as I go along.

"...but Cinderella couldn't go to the royal ball because she didn't have a dress."

"Why?"

"Because she couldn't afford one?"

"Why, Daddy?"

"Well, because she was on crack."

She really likes it when Goldilocks gets caught playing the PlayStation of the three bears, and instead of huffing and puffing, the big bad wolf cuts a giant fart and blows the house down. It's really triumphant if I can work a real one up for the special effects punch line. This always dazzles her. She must be proud.

When she finally passes out it's time to coerce the older two to climb into bed and let me read them a story so they can go to sleep. We get into bed but the pajamas they've chosen are too hot or too cold or too constricting and need to be changed. Once they've settled down and have got up to go pee a hundred times and have everything they need, they insist I make up a bedtime story, but not the same one as last night, it has to include them and all their friends from school, and it has to be a wild adventure and a little bit scary, but not too scary, and it has to be funny and have a happy ending with them dancing with a prince, and it can't be short, it has to be long and really good, and then pretend there was someone without a leg and that it got cut off somehow and now they have a wooden leg, and they're an orphan.

Eventually I'm not telling the story because they're just going on and on about castles and royal princes and people getting their heads chopped off until finally one says, "Like that, tell us one like that."

I do this verbatim and tuck them in and kiss them good night, but if you think this is where it ends you are dead wrong. We've just gotten started. The next hour and a half will be full of all the reasons why one of them has to get out of bed and come into the living room and tell me why she can't fall asleep, and that I need to check the closet for monsters, and there's a weird noise coming from under the stairs, and she thinks she felt a spider in her bed, and she needs a drink of water, and her nose is stuffy, and what if you and Mom die, and where does God really live, and what does He look like, and is there a separate place for goldfish and hamsters and other pets in heaven, and isn't it crowded then, and who cleans up after them, and it just goes on and on until we're both so exhausted she just falls asleep in the hallway somewhere.

Some parents I know have kids who just put themselves to bed without any fuss whatsoever. They probably get to watch a lot of television. I'm jealous. We devised a plan where we set an exact bedtime and what needs to be done before this agreed-upon time, and if things are carried out properly, they are allowed a half hour of TV after dinner; if not, they get nothing. This usually works for a few nights, but then a basketball practice runs late or there's a weekend sleepover where they stay up until midnight telling ghost stories and we're right back at ground zero. Until they're putting themselves to bed every night, I don't see a lot of television in my future.

At nine-thirty Jennifer gets home. I lie and tell her everything went fine and the kids went right to sleep. I grab a hat and a jacket, kiss her good-bye, get in the car, and drive off to Hollywood to play the show feeling like I should be back in bed myself.

I usually get to a show about five minutes before we play and don't hang around any longer than I have to. I'm not complaining, and certain people are going to read this and think I'm an asshole, but the whole preshow center of attention thing has become kind of a drag for me. Sounds stupid, I know, because why would you be in a band if you don't want attention, but I'm jaded and lame now and that's just how it is. There are parts of the whole show night interaction that I like a lot. I love talking to fans who are genuinely appreciative of our music and it doesn't matter how many times you hear it, it's great when someone tells you your music changed their life and is honest and sincere about it. I could hear that all night. I love seeing my friends who, year after year, come out and support our band through good times and bad, and it's always fun to have your crew around, hanging out and laughing at each other. I like shooting the shit with people from other bands and crew guys and finding out where they've been on tour and where they're going next, and what kind of guitars they play, and what music they've been listening to, and when they're working on a new record. I also like talking shop with people from the label who work for the band to see who they're signing and who's been fired or hired recently, but for all the great stuff around the show, there's a dark side as well.

When you're a singer, or actor, or radio host, or even the guy announcing the local little league game, basically anyone who puts themselves out into the public eye, you unknowingly open yourself up to pointed criticism from everyone from your best friend to complete strangers. Someone with horrible beer breath will come up to you and say they love your band but they like the old stuff better and didn't really care for the last few albums, and "what's with the third song on the new album, that song sucks, and why don't you guys play more like (insert stupid band here) and what time are you guys on tonight, and can I get a backstage pass for my girlfriend's cousin, and are there any more beers in your dressing room, because I looked and someone already drank them all, and bro, could you get me a shirt for my little brother? He really loves you guys, but like I said, he wasn't really that into your last record, either, and by the way, who did your last video? That thing was so gay! What was it even supposed to be about anyway? You guys should go back to playing super-fast like you did on your first album, and write more songs with words like 'fight' and 'fuck' in them 'cause that's cool, like 'fuck authority,' that's awesome. Yeah, dude, and don't forget, back-stage pass for my cousin and a shirt for my brother. Oh, and a hat for me, too. Thanks, bro. You rule."

I'll meet ten people exactly like this on the way into the club, there will be twenty more in the dressing room drinking all our beers and eating our deli tray, and thirty more on stage drunk when we play. Some of them, and this is no lie, will come out onto the stage in the middle of a song while I'm singing and yell in my ear, "Dude, are there any more beers left? Hey, and play song four off the second album, I forget what it's called." If you're physically unable to give them five extra laminates and a wristband for their girlfriend's cousin, a shirt for their little brother, and a few dozen beers, and if you won't party with them until dawn, well, then you're an asshole and your last album sucked.

What makes this irritating is that pretend you're a regular Joe working at the bank or at a construction site, and all day long, from the moment you get out of your truck, a never-ending stream of various drunken people were all over you, saying you used to be a good bank teller but now you suck, and can you run over to the Coke machine and buy them a soda, and hey, why don't you lend them your work belt because their girlfriend needs one, and bro, what about a free roll of quarters for their cousin, and would you please fill out the check slip the way they like it filled out instead of how you're doing it, and "How come you put up dry wall like that, *are you gay?*" Imagine if that was what your day was like every day. You'd begin to hate some people and feel a little jaded, and you'd show up to work about five minutes before your shift and not hang around one second more than you have to. There are a lot of nice people in the world you'll never meet, but the assholes will come up and prove it to you all the time.

The actual show itself goes well except a fight breaks out in the front row and some guy gets about three golf ball-size lumps on his head from this dude who looks like a cage fighter let loose from the county jail that very afternoon. The lighting guy thinks he's in Studio 54 and he's running crazy pulsing strobe lights and colored lasers all night like we're playing at a rave instead of where we are, which is East Hollywood, and he has a fifty-thousand-watt spotlight, like from a lighthouse, trained on me and blinding me in the eyes the whole time, and the best part, some clown is intermittently spitting on me from the front row. He has apparently confused me with someone in the Sex Pistols or UK Subs who sees this gobbing custom as a visceral appreciation for my fine performance. I see it as fucking incredibly gross and almost want to pull a Celine Dion and walk off stage. If you were walking down the street and some guy spit on you, either you're going to break his face or call the nearest cop and have him arrested for assault, but at a punk show it's considered a compliment. I could jump in after him and do an Axel Rose and have him sue me for my house, but at a certain point you think, I'm forty years old, I just put my kid to bed a half hour ago, I'm really not in the mood for a brawl in the mosh pit right now.

This spitting episode brings up another unfortunate misconception about punk: the gross factor, and no one has propagated this myth further than our guitar player. His milieu, however, is vomit instead of spit. He likes to cram his finger down his throat and throw up on people. This stunt is incredibly funny to him and gets great big belly laughs each of the three hundred hilarious renditions of the story are told from those who are entertained by this type of thing, but I imagine for the barfed upon as opposed to the barfer, it's less amusing. There's adolescent humor and then there's punk humor, which is apparently several levels down on the comedic evolutionary scale. Scatological tales, booger eating, and vomit are the tools of the trade for some of these punk rock jackasses who make some of the preschoolers I know look like models of stately class and maturity. Some people have confused the rebellion and social anarchy championed by punk as a carte blanche to act like Neanderthals and morons, but then again, I just told a story to my two-year-old that had me farting out the ending.

So I try to avoid the spitter's area of the crowd and we play the rest of the show, the kids go nuts and crowd surf and sing along, I play so hard and freak out that I sweat through my clothes and come off stage soaking wet, because, regardless of how jaded I am, I still believe in this shit. I believe in every word I sing, songs about feeling powerless against a world seemingly bent on self-destruction, about not fitting in with the perfect people constantly judging me, about wanting to leave regrets behind and live life deliberately and clinging to some small bit of hope that things could somehow change for the better even against mounting evidence to the contrary, and hearing this and feeling the same way, the crowd responds and sings along with us and it devolves into a writhing mass of humanity and we have that great cathartic release of pent-up aggression and frustration with the psycho world closing in around us, and that one moment reminds me of why I do this, why I put up with all the bullshit and criticism and maniacal guitar players and people wanting to package, market, and sell the last bit of dignity and self-respect I have left, and it's because it tells me I'm not alone in feeling this way and maybe that's what might make it okay, but the second the last chord is struck, I'm done. I'm my real self again, and I'm in the car and back on the freeway before most of them have left the building.

I come home and just want to watch some Conan O'Brien and go to sleep because my voice is already starting to feel hoarse and my muscles and bones ache and it's only the first show, so I go into the living room and lay down on the couch and wait for the buzz of the show and the ringing in my ears to subside so I can drift off and get some rest and then do it all again tomorrow night and every night again for the next three weeks. All of a sudden I hear a faint, "Daddy?" It's daughter number one, the drama queen. It's nearly two o'clock in the morning. What could it be now? A monster in the closet? A vampire under her bed? Another four years of a Republican-led Senate?

"I want some water, my throat hurts."

I get her the water and usher her back to bed, but she reappears by my side a few moments later.

"Daddy, I just can't sleep. I don't know what it is. I don't like my bed. My brain won't go to sleep."

I get insomnia too but after putting her to bed for three solid hours earlier I know she's tired and it's just her will toward dramatics that's moved her out of her bed and into the living room to interrupt me and my Conan time. About three more times I have to put her back into her bed and lay with her but she keeps shuffling back in a few moments later. Now she wants more water and keeps saying her throat feels funny and she's shivering. I offer to give her some cough syrup, or a throat lozenge or even a warm brandy and a cigarette, anything to get her back to sleep, but she keeps getting out of bed and going into the bathroom and drinking water.

At this point I should have known better that it wasn't her throat that hurt. She's always had this pathological fear of throwing up ever since she had one bad case of the stomach flu when she was younger, where she threw up so much she had to go to the hospital, an experience that apparently left her emotionally scarred and scared to death of vomit, her own or anyone else's. If anyone pretends to be sick, or feigns being about to hurl, even on TV, she'll clasp her hands to her ears and run screaming hysterically from the room, thinking it's contagious and she'll soon start barfing too. It's funny to everyone but her. Once her teacher was pregnant and had morning sickness and every once in a while would put her hand to her mouth and run to the door. My poor daughter would jump down and hide under the desk like it was an earthquake drill.

Sure enough, she goes to the bathroom and pretty much the moment I start to think, "Hey, maybe her throat doesn't hurt, and her stomach's upset, but she doesn't want to admit it because why else would she be out of bed at two in the morning," is right when I hear her first beginning to throw up into the sink, and then on the floor and the cabinets, the toothbrushes, the washcloths, the Sponge Bob nightlight, everywhere. She's basically projectile vomiting her hot dogs and cottage cheese all over the entire bathroom.

So I help her into some new jammies and she's a wreck of self-pity and lamentations for what she and I both know we're about to go through, which is about six hours of puke sessions every twenty minutes or so until she's dry-heaving into a Tupperware bowl at dawn's early light. Once she's comfortable I get to approach the wonderful chore of decontaminating and disinfecting the bathroom triage area that's now covered in partially digested hot dogs, cottage cheese, carrot chunks, and gross-smelling muck, so the rest of the family doesn't walk through it in the morning and get the stomach flu as well. While I'm on my knees with rubber gloves and my bucket of Lysol, trying to coax a piece of what looks like hot dog or carrot out of a crack of ceramic floor tile with a toothbrush, I start to wonder what other semifamous rock singers would be doing after a big L.A. show.

Maybe they'd get a couple of groupies and head back to the exclusive hotel on the sunset strip, sympathetically bringing along one of their kid brothers to provide him with a lifelong thrill so he can stroke his ego asking him intricate questions about how he came up with that one incredible riff on song four off the third album. He'd answer modestly, "Oh, I don't know. You can't really analyze where something that great comes from. You just have to be receptive to your creative flow and reach out and pluck it from your stream of consciousness and then mold it into your own mosaic so it touches something within the human spirit," pausing for effect before he does another line off a stripper's ass, and then kicks him out of the room. Yeah, that'd be great.

No, instead I'm cleaning barf off the bathroom floor at 2 A.M., and the little chunk of hot dog just keeps receding deeper into the crack in the ceramic tile. I prod, poke, and wedge but the damn piece of puke won't be released. Now it's become a test of will. Finally after much struggle, I manage to loosen the wretched speck and the bathroom is again free of bile and contaminant. I take off my rubber gloves and sit back on the couch and start to think of all the free beer, illicit drugs, and cheap sex that's being voraciously consumed just a half an hour's car ride away, just as daughter number one begins her second round of projectile vomiting next to me. She tries but misses the bucket I'd provided for her and covers the carpet with more hot dog parts and cottage cheese. I sigh and realize happily, I wouldn't change a thing.

TEENAGERS FROM MARS

I was at a local surf shop trying to find a hat to hide my receding hair line from my adoring fans, when I overheard the following conversation between a blond teenage girl wearing micromini gym shorts and a sweat jacket from our local high school, and her mother, a weary-looking bottle blonde business executive or real estate agent.

> **TEENAGE GIRL:** "Can I *please* stay at Stacy's house tonight?"
> **WEARY MOM:** "The answer when you asked me earlier was already 'No,' and if you keep pestering me about it the answer will be 'No' again tomorrow night."
> **TEENAGE GIRL:** "God, what crawled up your butt-hole?"
> **WEARY MOM:** "Now you're grounded for a week."

Adolescence has traditionally been viewed by classroom psychologists like something out of one of those films made in the 1950s we used to have to sit through in health education class:

"Still dependent on the safety and security of home life, but eager to cut their emotional umbilical cord and stake out their own independent identities, teenagers engage in a constant battle with the conflicts brought on by their base impulses and surging hormones. They seem to think, feel, and perceive things more intensely, becoming preoccupied with their appearance and reputation, and experiencing chaotic mood swings between raging, emotional outbursts and endless bouts of boredom and despair. They feel misunderstood and confused by their incompatible urges to walk the straight and narrow path, but to also cut loose and rebel. At school they struggle to find a group to fit in with among the segregated cliques of jocks, nerds, stoners, brains, and party animals, or worse yet, be cast out, unaffiliated, into loner status. If you are lucky enough to find a group that accepts you, the relentless pull of peer pressure can force you into any number of compromising positions and embarrassing conflagrations that you will play over in your mind for the rest of your life. In fact, much of your middle age will be spent recovering from it."

The problem with this description is that it defines pretty much everyone I know, no matter what age they are, which is, of course, the problem itself. In the past, parents have treated teenagers as pubescent hormone-crazed aliens, continually moving from one transitional "phase" to another, so we just write them off, deciding we won't be able to deal with them until they someday grow up and grow out of it. We see them all as stereotypical "teenagers," not as young people, and tend to treat them that way. This is why most of us couldn't get along with our parents in high school, because to them, we were hardly even human yet. They loved us, of course, but the generation gap was so wide, they couldn't possibly understand us, so why even try? Better to just ground us in perpetuity than unleash us on society when we weren't even close to being ready.

By the time I entered my teens I already had my punk rock attitude of defiance perfected, and it seemed like every day I was on a collision course with some form of trouble. My teachers had to disrupt class to keep me from talking out of turn, and most of the time I was either late or absent altogether. Some of it was good, clean, typical adolescent hi-jinx, like when I started a food fight in the cafeteria and got myself and several other classmates suspended for a week, but I also engaged in other more dangerous activities that could have proved tragic. Whenever I had the chance, I would steal alcohol and cigarettes from my parents' liquor cabinet, and by age sixteen, three times a week, after saying good night to my parents, my friend and I would sneak out of our bedrooms, take his mom's car and drive out to Hollywood to go to punk shows and nightclubs, and then drive wobbly home at 5 A.M., sleep for two hours, and then go to school. I finally was expelled from the junior prom for illicit activities and had to serve one hundred hours of sweeping up the school grounds before first period every day, or be shipped out to our rival high school. Throughout my entire teenage years I was a chronic screwup, and there were more than a few episodes where I could have ended up in jail or dead.

I often wonder if my parents could have said or done anything to help me. Probably not. I'm sure initially I would have refused any attempts for them to talk to me about sex, drugs, and alcohol issues, but if they persisted, I might have come around. I think young people want to be talked to like equals and leveled with. They may pretend they don't like to talk to adults, but that's usually only the case if the parent isn't really listening and is just trying to tell them what to do all the time. If my parents could have opened up a little and told me about some of the stupid things they did as teenagers, instead of the usual implied moral superiority, I might have seen them as more than just your stereotypical parental units whose soul purpose was to ground me and ruin my good time. Experience can be the best teacher, but a lot of times it's someone else's experience that teaches the best. If they were to tell me about their buddy who drank a fifth of whiskey and tried to pee out of a moving '56 Bel Air and had his left testicle ripped off, I might not have tried it from their '81 Volkswagen Rabbit. I probably would have, but at least we could have shared an amusing story.

For teenagers, the problem is that most parents, even if they are insanely wonderful and giving, can often become mortal enemies. It seems like they are the only two people in the world who constantly rain on your pubescent parade, and are capable of inspiring such extreme levels of embarrassment that you secretly pray they could somehow slip into a coma, wake up on Christmas Day, cut you a check, and then fall back into it. What was funny was that you could get caught stealing the *Mona Lisa* from the Louvre and taking a crap on it, and somehow it would be all their fault and you'd yell, "I HATE YOU!" and slam the door when they sent you to your room for it. There seems to be no way parents can win in this situation, and many of us feel like the best we can do is just hope to weather it somehow.

Probably the only way we'll be able to help our kids get through this time in their lives and remain somewhat close to them is if we try to reconnect with our inner punk rock adolescent, and remember to treat them as individuals, not just stereotypical melodramatic teenagers. I doubt it will be fun discussing certain topics with my daughters and just thinking about all the boy-friends I am going to have to meet and introduce to my sawed-off shotgun and my pit bull already gives me a migraine.

Regardless of how young at heart I pretend to be, I know the day will come when my daughters are embarrassed to have me around. I only hope they don't turn into those teens who just stop talking to their parents and treat them like furniture, or worse. Kids definitely won't be able to identify with the thirty-five-and-over you who worries about taxes and impending senil-ity, but they might be able to connect with the teenage you who started a pizza burrito food fight in the cafeteria and got every-one suspended and then felt bad about it. At some point I'll tell my teenage daughters about all the stupid things I did in high school and try and commiserate a little bit when they screw up the same way, instead of always being the implied moral author-ity and parental judge and jury. Maybe then they'll feel bad about telling people I am not their real father and pretend to want to hang out with me—at least for my wallet. This is one of the few ways I can imagine I'll be able to stay involved somewhat in their lives and not just be considered their allowance provider and weekend jailer.

"I'M JUST A SUCKA WITH NO SELF-ESTEEM. AWAAYYOOO!"

I remember at age fourteen or fifteen being on a constant search to find something I was good at. I tried surfing and skating, and although I had moderate skills, some of my friends at school were already sponsored by big clothing companies and win-ning contests. My other friends were star football and basketball players, but I never made it past the first two or three rounds of tryouts. Some friends were even on the track team, but by this time, I was already smoking half a pack a day so that was out. It wasn't until I was sitting there playing guitar in my room, like I did every day after school, thinking of what I could do that would interest me, that it suddenly came to me.

The active role I'll be able to take in helping boost our kids' self-esteem is never giving up in the search to find something that interests them. I can turn them on to music by buying them a secondhand guitar or drum set, get them involved in sports by taking them to basketball games or skate contests, or go down to the tide pools and try to get them interested in marine biology. If you haven't introduced your child to all these things in an endless search to help them find something they're interested in, you haven't done your job. People both young and old tend to judge their self-worth based on their looks and popularity, which are usually factors out of our control, but having something you enjoy doing and feel passionate about can sometimes be the only thing that makes you feel good about yourself and help steer you away from other more self-destructive impulses.

The test for us as parents becomes how we can help our budding adults learn to cope with their inevitable failures and disappointments, and encourage them not to give up hope. If we have bolstered their self-esteem, setbacks can seem like temporary opportunities to build character, not life-ending defeats. If we're able to remember what it was like to be an adolescent and treat our teenagers like real people, and not an age group, we should be able to better communicate with them and earn their admiration and respect. This way even if they do start listening to punk rock and decide that all figures of authority are worthy of contempt, they might at least let me pretend I'm on their side for a while.

I'M GONNA STAY YOUNG UNTIL I DIE

I love it when my kids call up a friend and ask if they can come over and "play." It's totally undefined. Just come over and we'll figure something out. We'll grab a ball and throw it at each other, or we can pretend we're astronauts who then become pirates who shoot each other's heads off and then have a tea party fashion show. Whatever! When there's a group of them together, like on my street where a clan of about eight kids travels in one huge prepubescent pack, they're like a child typhoon that storms through the area, careening from backyards to playrooms to driveways, front lawns, kitchens, and sidewalks. I'll be playing guitar in the garage and the door will burst open and they'll all come roaring in and grab the microphone and yell, "YEAH, YEAH, YEAH! ROCK 'N' ROLL! ROCK 'N' ROLL! COOL, DUDE! YEAH! YEAH!" and spaz out for a while doing crazy dances, then someone yells "LET'S PLAY TETHERBALL!" and they'll all scream "YEAH!" and go barreling out the door. Why is it that adults have to be totally drunk to act like this?

A while back I went to my nephews' school to engage in a game of kickball on Father's Day because their own dad, my wife's brother, had been called up by the Army Reserves to go to Iraq. I couldn't believe how much fun an innocent game of kickball could be, and a couple of innings into it I was right back on the grassy field of my youth booting home runs and beaning kids in the head with a big rubber ball when they tried to steal second. Sometimes I think we may have as much to learn from kids as they do from us about what's important in life.

Even though I turned forty last year, I still dress the same way I did when I was fourteen, Levi's 501s, Vans slip-ons, and a surf shop T-shirt and baseball cap. Most guys my age start dressing more age-appropriate and by now are wearing the suit and tie to work, and the Dockers and striped polo on casual Fridays. I know my dad doesn't still dress like the Fonz anymore, like his fading high school pictures suggest, with slicked-back hair, cigarettes rolled up in his sleeve, rolled-up jeans, and black penny loafers. As if I'm in some kind of perennial time warp, I still skateboard to the store to get milk and cereal for the kids' breakfast, and instead of golfing, I surf and skateboard. On our last tour of Europe, I cracked three ribs doing a stage dive at a music festival in Zurich. Let's just say I'm not Ozzie Nelson.

That being said, someone asked me recently what I thought of a new screamo band that was playing the Warped Tour this year, and I replied that it sounded like a bunch of screaming and noise to me. As the words were coming out of my mouth I realized what an old fart I sounded like, complaining about kids today and the racket they call music. I've also noticed a lot of my friends and I don't really listen to new music much anymore, preferring to listen to our old Clash and Ramones albums like old trusted friends, instead of worrying about keeping up with the latest trends. I imagine this is how it finally happens. We find that we can't relate to the kids anymore and the next thing we know we're wearing adult diapers and taking our teeth out and putting them in a glass of water on the nightstand every night.

I was also surprised to find my views on certain issues becoming more conservative in some ways. I'm not ready to start attending Republican fund-raisers at the local country club, but I do think that the increased glorification of violence, promiscuity, and drug use in films and music is having a negative impact on some young people. Video games about how great it is to be a pimp or a street thug, and DVDs about girls going wild have to in some small way affect their ability to distinguish right from wrong. Becoming a father has started making me take a look at some issues a little more differently. Many of our recent albums have had a strong political content in the lyrics, mainly because I was becoming concerned that the planet our kids would be inheriting would look like some kind of Orwellian nightmare, but populated by crystal meth–addicted pimps and hos.

Throughout the last century, the problem for many parent-child relationships has been what seemed to be an ever widening generation gap. Parents have always thought the music, fashion, and recreational activities of their kids were psychotic, irresponsible, and insane, and kids in turn found those of their parents hopelessly dull, old-fashioned, and boring. When I was listening to The Gears and The Germs, wearing Doc Martens and drinking from a beer bong for fun, my dad was listening to Frank Sinatra, wearing Hush Puppies, and playing golf. We were as different as the parents who saw Elvis Presley's singing a song about a 'hound dog' as the devil's music.

Somehow, over the last few decades, the generation gap seems to have narrowed somewhat. You see adults dressing like teenagers, and kids listening to Nirvana, Green Day, and the same bands their parents listened to when they were graduating high school. Punk rock, in all its nihilistic glory, somehow became the catalyst that helped close the generation gap, probably due to the fact that many of the people from our generation saw growing up and taking on responsibility as selling out and giving up, and have tried to hold on to their youthful outlook that much longer.

The closing generation gap actually presents a unique opportunity for our generation to create better relationships with our kids, and if we do it right, we could produce a generation of independent-thinking, conscientious young people, who could in fact stop repeating some of the tragic mistakes we've made in the past. If instead of forcing our religions, dogmas, and short-sighted way of thinking on them, we could encourage them to think for themselves, and show them how to be gracious and tolerant, rather than selfish and close-minded, maybe we could in fact make the world a better place, simply by being good parents. Wasn't this supposed to be the underlying goal of punk music in the first place, that we were to expose society for the sham it was, in the dim hopes of replacing it with a better one? Unfortunately, somewhere along the way we get caught up in the day-to-day struggle of ordinary life, and this becomes a lofty, unrealistic dream of utopia. There's a good chance we'll be so tired of chasing our kids around and keeping them out of trouble that we'll get lazy and just try and survive it all, and perpetuate the same problems we've always had in the past. Sometimes all we can do as parents is hope we've given the next generation the opportunity not to screw things up as badly as we have.

F@#K AUTHORITY?

"My daughter is at a school in a conservative area and she doesn't dress punk rock 'per se' but her attitude is all about doing her own thing and creating her own style. Some of the teachers and kids think it's kinda weird and she's gotten some flak from a teacher's aide in third grade who said what she was wearing wasn't appropriate for her age. It could be something as mellow as a Queen shirt with arm warmers. First of all, they are just a teacher's roadie, not a morality or fashion police. I told my daughter not to worry about that because sometimes when people are being creative and different and not conforming, it's not a bad thing, some people just don't understand. She took it personally like the teacher didn't like her but I told her the teacher didn't understand her and to just keep doing what she's doing."

—Greg Hetson, *Bad Religion & Circle Jerks*

When my daughter's teacher asked me on parents' night about my song on the radio, I was kind of embarrassed. What was a forty-year-old father of three doing singing a song about giving the finger to authority? Wasn't it being hypocritical to expect my kids to respect authority when I've been yelling at everyone not to?

As kids and teenagers we naturally wanted to rebel against our parents. Imagine if from the time you woke up in the morning to the time you went to bed, there were two giants hovering over you, saying, "Don't do that!" "Watch out!" "Don't touch that!" "Be quiet!" "Wear a jacket, or you'll catch a cold!" "Be careful, it's hot!" "Stop it!" "Time for bed!" Eventually you'd either (A) hate them with every fiber of your being or (B) want to do everything they're telling you not to do just to spite them, or more likely, both. After getting bossed around their whole lives, sometimes kids rebel just because they're tired of being told what to do all day.

Young chimpanzees and gorillas make faces and show their asses to their elders, but only when their backs are turned; they then revert to a submissive posture when the mature monkeys turn back around, kind of like when you used to sit in the backseat of the station wagon and make pig faces behind your dad's head. Rebellion is fun! We all like giving authority figures a piece of our minds when we think we can get away with it, whether it's flipping off the meter maid, sneaking past security to get into a show, or writing a punk song about sticking it to the man. Thumbing our noses at people in authority and derailing their power trips are how we take back some of the control for ourselves. Kids come with this impulse preinstalled, so it's up to us to know how to handle it.

In truth there are any number of reasons young people become rebellious, some just are total spazzes and can't help themselves, others just have a knack for wanting to be a pain in the ass. For my friends and me, when we were young we thought the rejection of all authority was what punk rock was all about. We spent all our time trying to prove society wasn't the boss of us. If the fashion of the day was preppy and conservative, we'd have green hair and torn clothes. If polite society decided what great art was, our music would be loud, fast, and obnoxious, and the imagery surrounding it deliberately decadent and offensive. It gave us independence from the other clones at school and a sense of self-worth, however damaged and depraved. Like the generations just before us that used rock music to distinguish themselves from their parents' taste and sensibility, we were staking out our own psychic territory where *we* made the rules, and decided for ourselves what was cool and what wasn't. What became known as punk rock and alternative culture arose out of the fallout of our generation's rebellious adolescent years.

As we got older we thought we could hold on to this youthful, idealistic state of mind, singing *"I'm gonna stay young until I die!"* at the 7 Seconds show and resisting the pressure to grow up and take on responsibility and wallowing in a state of perpetual adolescence. We thought that if we ever became parents ourselves, we'd be the coolest parents ever, letting our kids do everything our parents wouldn't let us do, like stay out all night and drink beer and smoke cigarettes and eat candy every day for breakfast. So what happens when we do become parents ourselves and the shoe is on the proverbial other foot, and we have little rebellious hellions of our own to bring up? Do we teach our kids to rebel against authority like we did so we're not hypocrites? Do we show them how to reject society's laws, live a life of anarchy, flip off cops, and join the Peace Corps?

I watched a TV show recently about a family where the parents let their children do whatever they wanted. The kids didn't listen to anyone, they acted and dressed in whatever way they saw fit, and came and went as they pleased. I've never seen three more disrespectful, obnoxious, maladjusted little brats in my entire life. They screamed at their mom when she would ask them to do the smallest thing. They hit, spit, kicked, and beat on each other, and generally ran around the house screaming like little pint-sized Napoleonic tyrants. Their mom and dad just shrugged and were okay with it because they wanted to be "cool" parents, and let them do whatever they wanted so they could "express" themselves. One of these so-called "cool" parents gave me my first bong hit when I was thirteen years old. She and her whole family smoked out together. After a few years of hanging out at their house every day after school, her kids and I all looked like miniature Keith Richards, stoned out of our minds. Sometimes trying to be the cool parent can do more harm than good.

The goal for us punk rock dads, then, becomes to somehow find a balance that will encourage our kids to question authority, but still respect us as their parents, even as unlikely as that sounds. I want to try to teach my kids to develop a healthy bit of skepticism so they're not easily gullible, because I think they need to be warned that some nefarious figures of authority aren't worthy of respect. Kids need to know that there are all kinds of different cults, religions, and dogmas out there trying to coerce them into accepting their sometimes highly fallible ways of seeing the world as fact, and that they should be wary of anyone trying to tell them exactly what to think and what to believe. They should also be encouraged not to always go with the in-crowd and cave in to peer pressure and not be afraid to express themselves creatively. The slogans of punk rock individualism and nonconformity are valuable guidelines when it comes to approaching the world philosophically, but we soon find out that when we have to face the harsh realities of the practical world, you need fewer slogans and philosophies and more common sense. So do we as punk rock parents teach our kids the bumper sticker mentality of "reject all authority" in every instance, even our own?

At a certain age we begin to realize that, like it or not, there are some rules that will keep you out of jail and out of trouble, and others that will keep you alive. We find out that our happiness— or at least staying out of really shitty situations—is eventually what becomes most important in life, and it's hard to be happy when you're in jail, on skid row, or dead. We all have tragic stories of friends and family members who without any discipline or respect for some of life's more appropriate rules ended up in extremely not fun places. So when your kid is playing in the front yard and bolts out into the street, you have the responsibility to show them that's a good way to become a human hood ornament. When they want to build a skate ramp to try and jump from your roof to their neighbor's, you can warn them that next time they'll probably be trying it in a wheelchair. You tell them that as much as you, too, would like to storm the Rampart Division, Congress, and the White House, and grab people by the lapels and take them to task for using the American Dream like toilet paper, the Constitution has included ways of doing this that won't get you brought up on federal charges. Even though you might have done it yourself, you also need to teach them that smoking dope and stealing cars for a living are great ways to make sure you become someone's bitch in prison. This is your duty and responsibility to your kids, no matter how cool and punk rock you think you are.

The balance between being the cool parent and the figure of fair and just authority is the balance beam all parents have to learn to negotiate; lean too far one way and you're the overbearing asshole always yelling at their kids until they can't have any fun, and lean too far the other way trying to be their best friend and your kid grows up with no discipline until life teaches it to them the hard way. This latter travail is even tougher for a parent from the Gen X punk scene. We feel so close to our own psycho adolescence, where we wanted to do anything to piss off our parents, and remembering what maniacal taskmasters our parents were and how we hated them for it, that now we overcompensate by trying to be the supercool parent.

Respect for authority needs to be earned. My kids will hopefully respect our authority as long as we set a good example and treat them like human beings instead of little cretins to be molded into whatever image we think they should be shaped into. They're still going to test the boundaries daily, it's in their genes. A parent becomes cool by considering their kids' point of view and by remembering back to when we were little punks and how shitty it felt when no one gave a crap about our opinions. When you have to lay down the law, you do it by setting boundaries beforehand, explaining the reasons why things are the way they are, and then doling out consistent humane discipline so they can learn a lesson they won't have to repeat a hundred times. If I can somehow manage this, maybe then they won't one day write a song about what a terrible dad I was.

MUSIC HISTORY 101

"You gotta play punk rock for your toddler. My daughter is two and she loves the stuff, but it really depends on who it is. She hates the first Suicidal Tendencies record, but she loves the new Sum 41. She hates David Bowie, but she loves Filthy Thieving Bastards. She hates None More Black, but thankfully she loves NOFX (well, not our new record so much, but she sure likes *War on Errorism*, though). You gotta play the punk for your kids early so they can have something to rebel against when they're older. As long as she doesn't start to like hip-hop, I'll be happy."

–Fat Mike, NOFX

When the second wave of punk music was going strong in the mid to late 90s, it was also the beginning of the boy band and pop music starlet era in which Britney Spears and *NSYNC ruled the modern radio charts and MTV. I considered it my duty as a punk rocker to ridicule their music as mindless drivel at every show we played, using our song "Perfect People" to launch into a tirade against lip-synching, sugar-coated, bubble-gum synth-pop performed by freshly scrubbed, impossibly attractive celebu-tantes that I saw as ruining American music. Now that I have kids who listen to this type of music all the time, I have to admit I've softened my opinion somewhat. Pop music exists solely to entertain people. It's escapist and catchy and all the neighbor-hood kids love to sing and dance along to it and read *Tiger Beat* magazine and put posters of pop stars up on their walls. Who am I to deny them this pleasure or say that it's wrong? It's almost a rite of passage. At first, I thought I should preach to them about how this type of music was consumerist, plastic, formulaic pab-ulum, but why ruin their good time and make them listen to the angry, aggressive message music I've listened to all these years? Maybe they'll have a better attitude toward the world than I did from listening to too many Sham 69 records.

That being said, once they reach a certain age, I do feel it's my duty to give them a week-by-week musical education so they're exposed to all different kinds of music. I'll start with some classical music—your Beethoven, Bach and Brahms, basically anything that starts with a "B" and has violins, just to give them some culture and lay the groundwork—but then it will be straight to the blues. I'll play them some Robert Johnson, Leadbelly, Howlin' Wolf, Muddy Waters, Bessie Smith, and B. B. King while they're playing with their dolls, and I'll explain that the blues was about feeling low and sad, and that sometimes, playing songs about feeling low and sad somehow makes you feel better. The next week we'll listen to some jazz music with Coltrane, Miles Davis, Chet Baker, Charlie Parker, and Thelonious Monk, and we'll wear French berets and dark sunglasses while discussing Sartre and existentialism. Then I'll play them some country with Hank Williams, Woody Guthrie, Gene Autry, and Bob Wills. I'll tell them this was music played by simple, hard-working American country folk and that it was really good before it was co-opted by urban cowboys in two-thousand-dollar snakeskin cowboy boots and women's jeans singing about achy breaky hearts and not messing with Texas.

The next week will be devoted entirely to rock 'n' roll. I'll tell them that although many people consider Elvis Presley to be the King of Rock 'n' Roll that there was also Chuck Berry, Bill Haley, Buddy Holly, Little Richard, Jerry Lee Lewis, Carl Perkins, Gene Vincent, and many others who should be included along with him as the forefathers of modern rock music. I'll tell them that the kids of the 1950s immediately loved rock 'n' roll, but their parents hated it, saying it was the "devil's music." I'll try to convince them that no matter what type of music they get into as teenagers, I won't tell them it's the devil's music, as much as I secretly suspect that it could be. Later on I'll admit that Elvis truly was the King and we'll rent *Jailhouse Rock* and *Viva Las Vegas*, and eat fried peanut butter and banana sandwiches and when it's all over I'll send them to bed and shoot out the television.

Then we'll come to the precursors in the 1960s who, each in their own way, whether by their music, stage presence, lyrics, or attitude, contributed to what would later be known as punk rock. We'll play the Beatles, the Rolling Stones, the Who, the Doors, the Seeds, the Velvet Underground, and the MC5. I'll explain to them while they're seated in beanbags around me and wearing tie-dyed shirts and moccasins that while this period undoubtedly produced some of the most awe-inspiring, jaw-dropping pure rock moments of all time, it also ushered in the era of free love and uninhibited experimentation with drugs. This will be a perfect segue into a long, complicated, uncomfortable discussion about the dangers of both that will include graphic slideshows and embarrassing first-person narratives that will hopefully entice them to want to join a convent. I know some of my punk rock counterparts plan to let their kids learn by their mistakes, but I don't have the time, money, or mental fortitude to do this. I'm thinking coercion by intimidation and fear will be easier on all of us.

Then it will finally be time for early punk rock with the New York Dolls, the Dictators, Patti Smith, Television, the Ramones, and Blondie. I'll buy them their first CBGB shirt, but never, under any circumstances, will I let them wash it. This is one genre of music that won't take any explaining. I'll just put on *Road to Ruin*, turn it up as loud as the speakers will go, and let them go at it. Punk rock is spontaneous combustion. When I was about fourteen, I put the Ramones on the stereo for some of my friends who hadn't heard of them yet, and the room instantly broke out into a spontaneous slam pit before anyone knew what that was or had ever seen one. Kids love to roughhouse. Punk rock just gave it a soundtrack.

Next I'll play them some British punk with the Sex Pistols, the Clash, Generation X, the Damned, and the Buzzcocks. I'll teach them how to flip people off the British way by using a backwards peace sign, but then ground them if I catch any of them doing it. Then, it will finally be time for my personal favorite, California punk, with the Germs, Black Flag, the Circle Jerks, the Descendents, the Adolescents, TSOL, 7 Seconds, Social Distortion, the Dead Kennedys, and Bad Religion. I'll show them how to stage dive and what to do if you fall down in the middle of a circle pit. I'll tell them that this was music created by bored suburban kids just like them, and that if they ever feel frustrated and confused, that they can always start a band and write songs about it and that sometimes this can be better than thousands of dollars' worth of time spent on a therapist's couch.

After that, I'll fill it all in with some East Coast punk like Bad Brains, Agnostic Front, Minor Threat, and the Misfits, and then post punk, skate punk, hip-hop, and everything else—Sonic Youth, the Pixies, Nirvana, the Smiths, Hüsker Dü, Eric B. & Rakim, Grandmaster Flash, the Replacements, Green Day, the Offspring, NOFX, Rancid, Refused, etc.—basically everything left over in my album collection that isn't punk or simply there by reason of lame ironic comedy. I feel that it's my responsibility as someone whose life was completely altered, colored, shaped, and categorized by whatever music I was listening to at the time, to give my kids a little background on why music is so important to me, and how it almost comes to define who we are. Once I've done this, it's up to them what they want to listen to. If they hear "Hold My Life" by the Replacements or "Clocked In" by Black

Flag and still want to listen to the Britneys and Justins, I might be a little disappointed but, at the same time, I'm their parent, what do I know?

EVERYTHING TURNS GRAY

> Though wise men at their end know dark is right
> Because their words had forked no lighting they
> Do not go gentle into that good night
>
> —Dylan Thomas

The other day I was talking to the owner of our record label and complaining that the guys in the band are giving me a hard time about not touring as much now that I have a family. I can't go out on tour for weeks on end like I did when I was twenty-one and had no responsibilities. He understood but said the other guys who don't have kids probably still want to go out on tour and live it up and that all of the bands from our era were facing the exact same problem. The guys with families are starting to settle down, but the others are still clinging to the hope that they can make the ride last a little longer. He said, "This is the graying of punk rock. It's never happened before."

Punk rock as a musical form is entering its middle ages. Jazz and blues are old and gray and staring mutely at a TV in a nursing home. Rock 'n' roll is a senior citizen eating at Sizzler and shouldn't be behind the wheel of an automobile. Hip-hop is approaching thirty, rolling in the dough but starting to look for tax shelters, and emo and screamo are young teenagers driving by us with their ass hanging out the window. A lot of us graying punk rockers are sitting around looking at each other, saying, "What happened?"

The issue becomes how do punk rockers get older and keep their edge and youthful idealism but still hold on to their dignity. To me it's starting to feel strange to be my age with three kids and a mortgage and life insurance and singing songs about not wanting to grow up and be responsible. It's a little late for that. It seems I have more hairs coming out of my ears and on my back than I do on my head nowadays, and what I do have up on top is rapidly becoming flecked with gray. The crow's feet around my eyes and wrinkles on my forehead are inspiring long, somber gazes into the mirror and more reflections on my mortality than I'd like to admit.

I don't want to be one of these guys in their sixties still wearing their leather jacket with NECROS spray-painted on the back and dying their gray hair orange in a vain attempt to convince themselves they still got it, that they're still cool. Some punkers have this romantic notion that you need to wear the uniform forever to prove that you are punk for life and you're never giving up. I'm punk for life because I love the music and the message and because I grew up surrounded by the culture of punk kids listening to beautiful nihilism in our headphones. The songs and imagery are the touchstones of my youth, riding through the alleys of the South Bay on my skateboard in my jeans and flannel shirt, listening to Wasted Youth and not caring what the world thought of me. This is who I am. I don't need to prove my stripes to anyone. Still, holding on to it so dearly can get kind of pathetic, like seeing a guy in his forties wearing his little high school football uniform, crying into his beer on his front lawn, pining for lost glory.

The last time we played the Warped Tour for its ten-year anniversary, although our fans were still as supportive and rowdy as ever, you could sense a shift, that a certain portion of the crowd was waiting to see the next hot young band playing after us and was just sitting through our show watching the veteran punk band so they could get a close spot for the next younger act. That sucks. I remember every other year the bands being scared to death to play anywhere around us, when the king of hip-hop, Mr. Number One on the top of the charts, cut his show early because our fans were chanting "PENNYWISE!" so loud you couldn't hear him. Yeah, those were the days. I already can envision myself, old and fat, drinking a scotch and water by the pool in Palm Springs retelling that one to my golf buddies day after day.

But recognizing that you're not as young as you used to be doesn't mean you need to stop loving the music and believing in its ideals. Punk to me stood for independence and nonconformity, and was a constant source of strength for those of us who felt ostracized for whatever reason. It embraced and championed individualism, while also trying to inspire a populist idea of unity and brotherhood among like-minded misfits pushed out to society's fringe. Coming out of the 1960s, punk was also about standing up to religious and political tyranny, demanding civil liberties, and exposing the fakes and phonies of the establishment for the greedy money grabbers they were. Punk rock encompassed so many of the concepts deeply embedded in my value system that I could never grow out of it. The music and spirit of bands like the Clash and Ramones flow through my veins and define who I am, no matter how old I get or what clothes I have on my back. It's not a fashion or an age but a way of looking at the world and finding your place in it, and like country, rock 'n' roll, blues, and hip-hop, it's going to be around a long time, as long as someone isn't willing to settle for the status quo and has an amplifier and guitar to tell the world about it.

BACKYARD CAMPOUT

After witnessing the tragic events of recent years, like many people I've felt a vague dissatisfaction with the sorry state of the world always looming around in the background of my everyday life. Maybe it was more like the last several decades. I'm not sure what the problem was; some people might say I was borderline depressed, which seemed stupid since I have so much to be happy about and thankful for. I'm a lucky guy in many respects; I have a great wife and three wonderful kids, and a career that brought a modest amount of notoriety and admiration, but I'm also one of these pathetic bleeding-heart liberals who wishes the world could be like the perfect utopia of a John Lennon song. I'd read the newspaper every day and see stories about babies getting killed in drive-by shootings and innocent children caught up in any one of the armed conflicts around the world and before I'd finished my morning coffee I'd already be shaking my fist at God for creating a world like this.

My career was another thing that gave me a lot of stress and dejection. Like many people, I'm not easily satisfied, and no matter how much praise or rewards we received, I heard the voices of the critics the loudest, and was always envying those who had more success than we did. I've read all the Buddhist books and tried to digest the idea that life is like a climb up a mountain, and that most people spend their whole lives hurrying through it, in an all-consuming effort to reach the top, eyes focused on the prize, when in reality we should go slow and enjoy the scenery, and be happy with what we have, the whole stop-and-smell-the-roses idea. But as much as you want to live that way, it's difficult to stay appreciative of everything you have in life when you're caught up in the daily grind, and you're always looking over the fence at your neighbor's grass to see what kind of turf builder he's using that keeps it so much greener than yours. Shallow, ungrateful, and pitiful, I know, but lie and tell me you don't feel this way sometimes as well; it's only human.

Then the other day I woke up and my daughter said to me, "Daddy, I want you to play with me today. You never play with me anymore." It hurt hearing her say it, but it was true. I'd been so wrapped up in my career and my pseudointellectual development that I'd become just a participant in her upbringing, breaking up fights with her sisters and refereeing at the dinner table, trying to get them to stay seated and eat their peas. I wasn't a terrible parent, but I wasn't a great one, either. So I told her we would set up the tent in the backyard and camp out. We went and got some firewood, my daughters brought their sleeping bags and dolls into the tent, and we played shadow finger games, told ghost stories, and roasted hot dogs and marshmallows all night. After they couldn't keep their eyes open any longer and finally nodded off, I sat there and watched them sleep and thought to myself, This is what it's all about. This is how I can truly be happy. I can't change the fact that men continue to resort to war to resolve their conflicts, or that people choose to kill each other over some strange idea of a benevolent God choosing sides in all this carnage. You can't always change the world. But I can make sure to play with my kids every day, and try to make them laugh and smile. It's easy to do. My daughters will remember the time I set the tent up in the backyard and we camped out together as long as they live. It was a day that we had a great time playing together and being carefree. It's our duty as parents to increase the number and frequency of these moments and memories. It doesn't matter how much money we have or what the critics say or what others think of me. What matters is if I had a great time with my kids. There are no rules on how to do it right, just real life. Everything else is out of my control.

THE SLOW, CONSTANT DRAINING

I can understand now how some parents get so competitive, or overprotective that they begin to hover over their kids constantly, hoping to shield them from every kind of harm that might come their way. If there's one thing parents do well, it's worry. We know how cold and heartless the world can be, and how tragedy can strike at any time unannounced. There will be late-night car rides from parties to worry about, bad grades and missed goals, dateless prom nights and career setbacks, not to mention the heartless teasing and name-calling that cuts deeper than if it was you yourself being wounded by it. Then one morning, you wake up and you're middle-aged, and it seems the whole world has passed you by. In our kids we see our lost youth, and that naïve sense of hope and innocent wonder at the world, where even when it felt like the weight of it all could crush you, at least you knew you were alive, and ascending.

So now when he gets a free moment the Punk Rock Dad goes into the garage and plays his guitar. He plays in the morning, and late at night, and at strange times in between. He plays a '78 black Les Paul Standard through a Marshall JCM 800, because only a poser would play through anything else, and there is absolutely no need whatsoever to play through anything other than a JCM 800 if you are holding onto a black Les Paul Standard. He plays extremely loud to the point of perturbing the neighbors and making backyard dogs howl, and there is feedback, and distortion and velocity that echoes throughout the house and shakes the rafters on the low E notes. The dog covers its ears, the cat hides, and the children turn up the television to try and drown out the sound that won't be drowned out, and the wife, in vain, pretends not to hear it, but Punk Rock Dad strums away for hours on end, writing songs no one may hear but himself, odes to his frustration with the way the world is, but also to the nihilistic spark of life that boils inside him, that at certain times makes him want to get in his car and drive extremely and dangerously fast, to go outside and knock the hat off the first person who looks at him in a way he doesn't like, to the Gods and fables that have foisted this world upon him. He plays until his fingers bleed and shoulders ache, songs about love, hope, fear, joy, redemption, heartache, and death, and the songs never end, but begin to blend into each other, until they are one long connected symphony of pain and release, a tribute to being alive and dead at the same time, an opera of blood, sweat, and tears, of nothing-ness and everything, and the song is still going, still being played at criminal volume, in garages, and small towns. It has become the music of the spheres reverberating between the planets and echoing across the universe. For him, it becomes the song of life and the slow, constant draining of it, one that before had seemed pointless and currupt, but is now filled with purpose.

ACKNOWLEDGMENTS

I would like to thank Matthew Benjamin at Collins for his immeasurable patience, hard work and help in putting this book together and for taking a chance on the lead singer of a punk band who thinks he can write. To Caroline Greeven and Marc Gerald from the Agency Group for coming up with the idea for the book and believing that I could pull it off against all evidence to the contrary. To Andy Somers, our long-suffering booking agent, for suggesting me as an author. To the supportive team at Collins: Joe Tessitore, Mary Ellen O'Neill, Jean Marie Kelly, Ginger Winters, George Bick, Teresa Brady, Felicia Sullivan, and Marina Padakis. To the other punk rock dads, Joey Cape, Tony Adolescent, Noodles, Fat Mike, and Greg Hetson for their quotes, and to Crystal Lafata for helping me track them down and force them to do it. To Kat Monk for taking the cover photo. To Steve Carranza for the insane drawings of the Anarchy Bottle and Mommy's Little Monster. To myself for doing all the other images and to Sunil Manchikanti for assembling them all. To Amy from KROQ for being cool. To Brett, Gina, Andy, Dave, Jeff, and everyone at Epitaph for putting up with us for nearly two decades. To Fletcher, Byron, Randy, and the worldwide PW crew for letting me have the back lounge on the tour bus in Europe to work on the book, and for being the best band and crew in the world. To my mom and dad for not grounding me half as much as they could have, and for just being two great people anyone would be proud to call parents. To my sister and all the Johnsens for being awesome and to our entire extended family. To all the punk bands who got me through my adolescence. To my friends who tried to understand why I stayed home to work on the book when the waves were good. And most of all, to my wife, Jennifer, and to Brighton, Emma, and Kate, for giving me something to believe in.